Moments That Take Your Breath Away

JAMES W. MOORE

Moments That Take Your Breath Away

Abingdon Press
Nashville

MOMENTS THAT TAKE YOUR BREATH AWAY
by James W. Moore

Copyright © 2008 by Abingdon Press

All rights reserved.

This book is printed on acid-free paper.

Library of Congress Cataloging-in-Publication Data

Moore, James W. (James Wendell), 1938-
    Moments that take your breath away / James W. Moore.
        p. cm.
    ISBN 978-0-687-49069-1 (pbk. : alk. paper)
    1. Spirituality. 2. Christian life. I. Title.

    BV4501.3.M66425 2008
    248.4--dc22

                                                    2008001549

08 09 10 11 12 13 14 15 16 17—10 9 8 7 6 5 4 3 2 1
MANUFACTURED IN THE UNITED STATES OF AMERICA

For Mason Joseph Moore

CONTENTS

INTRODUCTION:
THE BREATHTAKING
MOMENTS OF LIFE

*H*ow long has it been since you had one of those moments that takes your breath away? As we have been reminded in numerous ways in recent years (through billboards, banners, plaques, bumper stickers, church bulletins, and so forth), "It is not the number of breaths we take, it is the number of moments that take our breath away." And this is so true! Life is so much more than an endurance test. It is so much more than "tick-tock time"—time measured by the ticking of a clock, with each second exactly like the one that preceded it and the one that follows it. No, every now and then—and more often than we realize—God breaks into the routine and gives us one of those awesome moments, so powerful, so amazing, so beautiful, that "time seems to stand still." It's a moment that takes our breath away!

This is what happened to Isaiah in the Temple (Isaiah 6). He came to the Temple that day as he had come routinely so many times before, but on that day he "saw the Lord high and lifted up." It took his breath away, and he accepted God's call to be a prophet. He heard God's call, "A prophet is needed for this hour"; and with breathtaking excitement, Isaiah responded, "Here am I; send me" (verse 8).

This is precisely what happened to Moses in Exodus 3. Moses was watching over his father-in-law's flock one day, as he had so many days before, when all of a sudden God appeared to him in a burning bush. Moses was so inspired by that breathtaking moment that he took off his shoes, because he knew this was a sacred moment and he was standing on "holy ground" (verse 5). And from that moment, he set out to go to Egypt and set God's people free.

And look at Jesus. Jesus in his lifetime on earth inspired so many breathtaking moments. All kinds of images come to mind:

- the shepherds and the wise men, kneeling in awe and wonder at the manger;
- the elders in the Temple, amazed and astonished by the wisdom and insight of the twelve-year-old Jesus;
- Zacchaeus, up in a sycamore tree, so bowled over by Jesus' acceptance of him that he comes down out of that tree giving money away;
- Bartimaeus on the Jericho Road, healed of his blindness by Jesus, so inspired by Jesus' goodness and power, that he drops everything and follows Jesus on the way;
- the woman in the crowd who touched the hem of Jesus' robe in hopes that this simple gesture could bring the healing she had been seeking for twelve long years; and when the healing does indeed come, she is overwhelmed by the love and power of Jesus in that breathtaking moment;
- Doubting Thomas in the upper room, who finally sees the risen Christ with his own eyes and falls in amazement on his knees, exclaiming, "My Lord and my God!";

- Saul of Tarsus, encountering the resurrected Lord on the Damascus Road, so blown away by God's amazing grace in that breathtaking moment that he is converted and becomes God's missionary to the Gentiles and the prolific writer of much of what we now call the New Testament.

We could go on and on, because Jesus' life was filled with moments that take our breath away. I am sure that right now you are thinking of many others, because there are so many. But the question is: How is it with you? How long has it been since you had a moment like that—a moment so powerful, so touching, so awesome, that it took your breath away? Some of the breathtaking moments are life-changing. All are inspirational!

I have had many moments like that. Some were quite dramatic, some were quite memorable, some were just too beautiful for words. Do you remember the first time you saw the ocean? Or a majestic mountain range? Or a breathtaking sunset with colors so amazing that you find yourself thinking, *Only God could do that!* Do you remember the fist time you saw the Statue of Liberty? Or a majestic cathedral? Or a rosebud? Or a stunning skyline? Or a rippling wheat field at harvest time? Have you ever had your breath taken away by the gracious generosity of a friend? Or the beauty of a loved one? Or the kindness of a neighbor? Or the unexpected support from someone in your time of trouble? Or the innocent face of a little child? Or the heart-touching impact of a Mozart concerto or a Bach anthem or a Dickinson poem or a powerful sermon?

God has so many breathtaking moments for us, but we have to have the eyes of faith to see them, the ears of faith

11

to hear them, the hearts of faith to feel them, and the hands of faith to seize and embrace and celebrate them.

It happened again for our family on August 16, 2007. We got our first look at our new grandson, Mason Joseph Moore (to whom this book is dedicated). He was born at 5:41 P.M. Twenty minutes later, we got to see him for the very first time. And as it had happened before with our two children and with our four other grandchildren, it was one of those amazing, incredible, powerful, awesome moments that took our breath away. There is nothing in the world like the miracle of birth, the miracle of life; and when you experience that in your own life or in the life of your family, it is absolutely breathtaking!

It is my hope and prayer that as we explore in this book the many different kinds of moments that take your breath away, we will celebrate the ones mentioned here in these pages. But also, I hope that we will think of many moments not mentioned here and, most of all, that we will all become more aware of and receptive to the myriad breathtaking moments that God, in God's amazing grace, has in store for us in these days and in the days ahead. May the love of God, the forgiveness of God, and the grace of God touch your heart as never before and take your breath away!

1

IT'S NOT THE NUMBER OF BREATHS WE TAKE, BUT THE NUMBER OF MOMENTS THAT TAKE OUR BREATH AWAY

Scripture: Psalm 118:19-24

*I*t had been some time since Jack had seen the wonderful older man who lived next door. Through the years, college, dating, career, the rush to success, and life itself had all gotten in the way. In the hectic pace of his busy life, Jack had had little time to think about the past, and now, often no time to spend with his wife and son. He was working on the future, and nothing could stop him.

But then came the phone call. It was his mother, and she said, "Mr. Belser died last night. The funeral is Wednesday." Memories flashed through Jack's mind like an old newsreel, as he sat quietly remembering his childhood days.

"Jack, did you hear me?"

"Oh, sorry, Mom. Yes, I heard you. It's been so long since I thought of him. I'm sorry, but I honestly thought he died years ago," Jack said.

"Well, he didn't forget you, Jack. Every time I saw him, he'd ask how you were doing. He'd reminisce about the many days you spent over on 'his side of the fence,' as he put it," his mother told him.

"I loved that old house he lived in," Jack said.

"You know, Jack, after your father died, Mr. Belser stepped in to make sure you had a man's influence in your life," his mother said.

"I know," Jack said. "He's the one who taught me carpentry. I wouldn't be in this business if it weren't for him. He spent a lot of time teaching me things he thought were important. Mom, I'll be there for the funeral."

As busy as he was, Jack kept his word. He caught the next flight to his hometown. Mr. Belser's funeral was small and brief. He had no children of his own, and most of his relatives had passed away.

The night before he had to return home, Jack and his mother stopped by to see the old house next door one more time. Standing in the doorway, Jack paused for a moment. It was like going back in time. The house was exactly as he remembered it. Every step, every picture, and every piece of furniture held warm and wonderful memories. But suddenly, Jack stopped.

"What's wrong, Jack?" his mother asked.

"The box is gone," Jack said.

"What box?"

"There was a small gold box that he kept locked on top of his desk. I must have asked him a thousand times what was in the box, and Mr. Belser would always say, 'Jack, in that box is the thing I value most these days,' but he never told me what it was." But now the box was gone. Jack and his mother decided that a member of the Belser family had taken it, and that they would never know what it was that was so valuable to Mr. Belser.

Jack flew back home and went back to work the next day. A day or so later, a package arrived in the mail for Jack. The return address caught Jack's immediate attention: It was Mr. Belser's name and address.

14

Jack ripped into the package. Inside was the gold box. His heart racing, Jack carefully opened the gold box, and inside he found a beautiful gold pocketwatch. Cautiously, he unlatched the cover. Inside, he found engraved on the watch cover these words: *Jack, thanks for your time! Harold Belser* Jack swallowed hard as he realized: *Oh my goodness, the thing Mr. Belser valued most was my time.* Jack held the watch in his hand thoughtfully for just a few minutes. Then he called his office and cleared his appointments for the next two days. "Why?" his assistant Janet asked. "Because," Jack said, "I need to spend some time with my wife and my son. And oh, by the way, Janet...thanks for your time!"

I like that story because it reminds us of a very important truth of life that we are so prone to forgetting in this busy, hectic, pressure-packed, competitive, success-oriented world in which we live, namely this: Life is not measured by the number of things we accumulate or the number of awards we win or the number of successes we achieve or the number of honors we receive or the wealth we pile up or the number of years we put in. No, in the final analysis, the bottom line is this: It's not the number of breaths we take, it's the number of moments that take our breath away.

Some years ago, the gifted writer Robert Raines was directing a retreat center up in the beautiful Pocono Mountains in Northern Pennsylvania. Early one morning, Robert Raines got into his car and started driving through the mountains. There was no one on the road at that time, as the mountains were quietly beginning a new day. The beautiful colors of autumn were splashed all over the trees. It was a magnificent, glorious, breathtaking sight as the early

15

morning sun glistened upon the wonders of the colorful mountains and the fragrant valleys stretched out beneath them.

And then it happened: Robert Raines saw one of the most beautiful things he had ever witnessed in his life. Right there, at the very edge of that great mountain peak and facing the gorgeous valley below, was a young man in his early twenties with a trumpet pressed to his lips, and he was playing the Doxology! With his lungs expanded fully and releasing all of the energy in his soul, he was standing there in the morning sunlight playing the Doxology on his trumpet! "Praise God, from whom all blessings flow; / praise him, all creatures here below; / praise him above, ye heavenly host; / praise Father, Son, and Holy Ghost" (words by Thomas Ken, 1674).

The point is clear: With all the stresses and problems and challenges in life, still the truth is we have so many "doxologies" to sing, so many blessings to count, so many things to be grateful for and inspired by. We have so many moments available to us that can absolutely take our breath away, if we have the eyes of faith to see them, the ears of faith to hear them, the hearts of faith to feel them, and the grace to celebrate them. This is precisely what the psalmist was talking about when he said, "This is the day that the LORD has made; / let us rejoice and be glad in it" (Psalm 118:24).

Now, I want to ask you do something. Blank out your mind for a moment (that's real easy for some of us), and now think of the moments in your life that were breathtaking— the moments that absolutely took your breath away.

Well, what did you come up with? A magnificent sunset? Or a glorious sunrise? The waves billowing in from a beautiful blue-green ocean? A peaceful farm covered with new snow? The creative genius of a Broadway play? A majestic church spire pointing us toward God? Or your first look at your newborn baby?

All of those came to my mind, and they all touched my heart powerfully, but I also thought of those incredible moments, those amazing moments in our personal relationships that are so wonderful and so moving that it seems like time stops and "time stands still," just for the celebration of that moment.

I have had hundreds and hundreds of these moments—and I'm sure you have too—but for now let me lift up just three. They are all very personal, because all breathtaking moments are very personal.

First of All, There Is the Breathtaking Moment of Love

It happened a few years ago. Our grandson Paul was showing me what he could do on his computer. He was just four years old at the time, and already he was using a computer.

He had a Tonka Toy CD, and he put it in the computer. Then on the screen, he was showing me how he could use a bulldozer to build highways through the desert; a snowplow to clear icy roads in the mountains; and even a helicopter to build bridges across a canyon. It was fascinating to watch his mind work and his little four-year-old hand move the computer mouse to get the results he wanted.

As he continued to play his computer game, we got into a man-to-man conversation. I said, "Paul, are you still enjoying school?"

"Yes sir."

"Do you have lots of friends at school?"

"Yes sir, I do."

Then I said, "Paul, who is your best friend?"

17

Paul stopped playing his computer. He turned and looked me square in the eye, and he said, "YOU!"

Oh, wow! What a breathtaking moment that was, a cherished moment of love that will stay with me forever. That look in his eyes, that tone in his voice said it all: "Gran, don't you know? You are my best friend!" I didn't see it coming, but that moment of love—so pure, so innocent, so genuine, so wonderful—took my breath away.

Let me ask you something: How long has it been? How long has it been since you had a moment of love like that, a moment of love so powerful that it took your breath away?

Second, There Is the Breathtaking Moment of Gratitude

It was a Thursday night in the spring of 1996. We were in Donaldsonville, Louisiana, hosting a rehearsal dinner for our son, Jeff, and his fiancée, Claire, who were going to be married the next evening. We enjoyed a sumptuous South Louisiana meal; and after the meal, we viewed a video about Jeff and Claire. When pictures of Claire's life were shown, the background music was "Brown-Eyed Girl," and then Jeff's history was depicted on the video screen, accompanied by that beloved, famous, classic ballad "Son of a Preacher Man"!

People laughed and applauded, and then the tributes began. Friends and family members stood in turn to reminisce with Jeff and Claire, to lovingly tease them, to express their friendship and support, to celebrate their love, and to wish them well.

It was a warm, wonderful, and intimate time. Then as the evening was wearing down, our son, Jeff, stood to speak. He spoke tenderly and lovingly about Claire; and then, speaking

18

directly to her, he gave a touching and moving tribute to the beautiful young woman who would soon be his bride. He thanked everyone for coming (from far and near) to share this special time with them. He spoke special words of love and appreciation to his sister, Jodi, and to her husband, Danny. And then, he turned toward his mom and dad, and he said words we will never forget. He pointed toward us, and he said, "If I lived thirty lifetimes, I could never fully express my gratitude to my family for all they have done for me."

The words he said, and the way he said them, were so powerful that you could have heard a pin drop in that crowded room; and for a moment (just a brief moment), time stood still, because those words of gratitude took our breath away.

As we looked at Jeff and his sister, Jodi, through misty eyes and realized what great Christian adults they had become, I remember thinking: *If we lived a thousand lifetimes, there is no way we could ever fully express our gratitude to God for the joy they have given us.* And on top of that—talk about breathtaking moments—they have now given us five amazing grandchildren!

Now, take it to a deeper level. If we lived a million years, we could never, ever fully express our gratitude to God for the gift of his son, Jesus Christ.

Let me ask you something: How long has it been since you had a moment of gratitude like that, a moment of gratitude so powerful that it took your breath away?

Third and Finally, There Is the Breathtaking Moment of Inspiration

It's that moment when you feel the presence of God closer than breathing, nearer than hands and feet—that moment when God breaks in and reminds you that he is

with you, and he will give you the strength you need. Someone once said, "God always gives us the strength we need at
the time we need it. He doesn't give it to us in advance, or
else we would take the credit!"

I have had so many incredible, breathtaking moments of
inspiration in my lifetime; but for now, let me share with you
one of the more recent ones. A few years ago, I went to
Methodist Hospital in Houston with my wife, June, to receive her fifth of six chemotherapy treatments. Up to that
point, all had gone perfectly, like clockwork. We would show
up on the appointed day. They would start June's treatment
(without a hitch) at 8:00 in the morning, it would conclude
at 5:00 or 5:30 in the evening, and we would go home.

But, when we showed up for treatment number five that
particular Monday morning, the nurse said, "I hate to tell
you this, but we may have a problem. Your blood work from
last Friday shows that at that time, your white count was
borderline, and we probably will have to postpone your
treatment. I will test your blood again to be sure, but really,
I don't think there is any way the white count will be up
enough to do the test, so you may have to go home and come
back next week."

Now, let me tell you something: When you go to receive
chemotherapy, you want to go on and do it and get it over
with. I didn't want June to be disappointed, so I began to say
to her, "You know, through this whole experience we have
learned all over again just to take one thing at a time. So, if
we can't do the treatment today, we'll just come back next
week. We'll just go with the flow." And June said, "I feel really good today. I really believe the blood test will be okay."

A few minutes later, the nurse came back smiling. She
had the chemotherapy supplies in her hands, and she said, "I
have never seen anything like this: From Friday to Monday,

your white count has *doubled*! This is amazing! It's unbelievable."

And June replied, "It's all of those prayers! We've got a whole church full of wonderful people praying for us, and this is just another one of those incredible experiences that we keep having over and over." And then June said, "I call it 'a God thing'!"

And she was right. I knew it was indeed "a God thing," and I just sat there and watched the Holy Spirit work. It was yet another moment of inspiration that took my breath away.

God has lots of breathtaking moments for us today—moments of love, moments of gratitude, moments of inspiration; because, you see, this is the day the Lord has made; we can rejoice and be glad in it.

2

The Moments When We Know We Are Standing on Holy Ground

Scripture: Acts 7:30-33

*B*ishop Janice Riggle Huie tells about an experience she had a few years ago that touched her heart. She was interviewing a group of ministerial students about their call to the ministry. She said to each of them in turn, "Tell me about your calling. What do you think God is calling you to do?"

Most of the students gave very practical answers, like, "God is calling me to be a hospital chaplain," or "God is calling me to be a teacher on the college level," or "God is calling me to be a counselor," or "God is calling me to be a pastor."

But then she came to one young woman who seemed a bit shy at first, not quite as bold as the others, and Bishop Huie said to her, "Tell me about your calling. What do you think God is calling you to do?" And the young woman said, "I don't know exactly yet where God will lead me. I just know one thing: God is calling me to introduce people to Jesus Christ!"

When Bishop Huie tells this story, she says, "At that moment, when I heard that young woman say that, I wanted to take off my shoes, because I knew I stood on holy ground."

Let me ask you something: Have you ever had a moment like that, a moment that was so powerful, so touching, so wonderful, so sacred, so breathtaking, that you wanted to take off your shoes because you knew you were standing on holy ground?

That's precisely how Moses felt that day as he stood before the burning bush. The bush burned but was not consumed, and in that experience Moses felt the presence of God and heard the voice of God and received the call of God.

There are three fascinating things to notice in this great and dramatic Bible story. First, we see that it was a surprise. It happened at a time when Moses least expected it; and it happened in a most unusual place, out in the wilderness. God's presence made that desolate place holy and sacred. This simply suggests to us to be ready. God can speak to us at any moment, maybe even when we least expect it.

Second, we see that in order for Moses and us to get it, to grasp the full meaning of an experience like that, reverence is required. This is something of a problem for us in our world today because the very opposite, irreverence, is the characteristic of our modern world. Very little is held sacred anymore in our contemporary society, and we wonder why we don't hear the voice of God more clearly or feel his presence more nearly. Is it because we have forgotten how to be reverent?

Third, we see that Moses had a seeing eye and a hearing heart. Breathtaking burning bushes are all around us; but we have to have the eyes of faith to see them, the ears of faith to hear them, and the hearts of faith to feel them.

In her work, *Aurora Leigh*, Elizabeth Barrett Browning describes how the whole creation is filled with God's wondrous miracles and how every bush is a testament of God's love and majesty and then she adds these two powerful lines: "But only he who sees, takes off his shoes, / The rest sit round it and pluck blackberries" (Oxford University Press, 1998; page 246).

The plain truth is that holy ground is all around us, because God is ever-present with us. If, in reverence, we have the seeing eye and the hearing heart; we can be well aware that God is reaching out to us and speaking to us loud and clear through burning bushes and sacred moments and holy ground right in our own back yard, right under our noses.

Let me show you what I mean.

First of All, There Is the Holy Ground of Service

As Christians, we are first and last called to be servants of God. We are not called to be prima donnas or celebrities or superstars. We are called to be humble, willing, self-giving servants of Christ.

Some years ago, a Christian Ashram was started in India. Converts would come there to learn the Christian faith. One convert who came to the Ashram was a Brahmin. You remember that the Brahmins were the upper class, the upper crust of society.

In this Christian Ashram, everyone present was expected to help with the community chores—to mop the floors, to wash the dishes, to serve the meals, even to clean the bathhouses. The former Brahmin came to the Ashram leader one day and announced that he could not possibly perform such menial chores. They were beneath him, he said. The Ashram leader told him that in Christ there are no menial tasks and that all good works are sacred, and that he should have no trouble as a Christian mopping floors and washing dishes and even cleaning bathhouses. When the Brahmin heard that, he said to the leader, "I'm converted, but not that far!"

Put that over against Mother Teresa, who simply pretended that every person she met was Christ in disguise. She served every person and performed every task as if she were doing it for Christ. And that's what it really means to be a servant Christian.

Some years ago I was invited to the campus of a small United Methodist college to be on a panel discussing Christian vocations. As we got started, those of us on the panel were asked to introduce ourselves by giving our name and our vocation. The introductions were rather routine, such as "My name is Mary Smith, and I'm a lawyer." "My name is Joseph Parker, and I'm an architect." "My name is Martha Brown, and I'm a mathematics professor." I was next, and I told my name and that I am a minister.

But then there was one final panelist, a doctor, and I will never, ever forget what he said. After stating his name, he said, "We are here today to talk about Christian vocations. Now, as I understand it, the word *vocation* means 'calling.'" He paused for a moment, and then he said, "My calling is to be a Christian, and one of the ways I do that is through the practice of medicine." When he said those words, I wanted to take off my shoes, because I knew I was standing on holy ground.

Wasn't that great, the way he put that? It took my breath away! "My calling is to be a Christian, and one of the ways I do that is through the practice of medicine." That was the holy ground of service.

Whenever or wherever we serve God, there is breathtaking holy ground. That's number one.

Second, There Is the Holy Ground of Love

Some years ago, I was surfing through the TV channels with my remote control when I hit the sports channel. A football player for the Kansas City Chiefs was talking about Coach Dick Vermeil. I was fascinated and touched by what this veteran professional football player was saying about Coach Vermeil. With great affection, he said, "I love Dick Vermeil, not only for what he taught me about football, but also for what he taught me about life." This tough football player had to blink back his tears and regain his voice; and then he said, "Coach Vermeil is like a father to me. He taught me a lot about football, but he also taught me how to treat the custodian with kindness and how to speak to the young man who picks up the dirty towels."

When I heard that, it took my breath away. I wanted to take off my shoes, because I knew that I was standing on holy ground, the holy ground of love and respect for others.

Have you heard about the man who fell into a deep manhole? He tried and tried but could not get out on his own, so he began to cry out for help.

A physician came by. He heard the man crying for help, so he wrote a prescription and tossed it down to the man. But the man was still in the hole.

A minister came by and heard his cry, so he wrote a prayer and tossed it down to the man. But the man was still in the hole.

Then the man's best friend came by. He too heard the man's cries, and (would you believe it?) the friend jumped into the hole with him.

The man said, "Why did you do that? Why on earth did you jump into the hole with me? Now we are *both* stuck."

"No, we're not," said the friend, "because I know the way out!"

This parable-story reminds us of how Jesus Christ jumps into the deep hole of our lostness and captivity so that he, in his love and compassion and amazing grace, can lead us out to freedom and new life.

That's the way Jesus Christ loves us—generously, sacrificially, graciously, unconditionally—and that's the way he wants us to love one another. And whenever and wherever we do that, we had better take off our shoes, because we are standing on breathtaking holy ground.

Third and Finally, There Is the Holy Ground of Sacred Responsibility

God didn't just appear to Moses in the burning bush; God gave him a job: "Go and set my people free! Go and bring my people out of Egyptian slavery. Go, and I will go with you!" God gave Moses a job, a sacred responsibility.

In the spring of 2006, my family and I were out in the courtyard of our church after the 11:00 A.M. service. I had just announced that we would be retiring in a few weeks, and people were coming by to hug us and wish us well in this new chapter in our lives. The people in our St. Luke's church family were always so amazingly thoughtful, so generous, so gracious, so loving; and we were touched by the kind words and tender hugs.

Toward the end of the line, a woman came and hugged us, and then she told me that her children had grown up in St. Luke's, how much the church had meant to them over the years, and how now they were all living in different places in the United States. Then, she said, "After 9/11, the children, independently of each other, all called, and they all asked, 'What did St. Luke's do, and what did Jim say?'"

Wow! That took my breath away. I was so touched by those words. A few minutes later, I went alone back into the sanctuary to retrieve my Bible, which I had left on the pulpit.

I stood there and looked at our amazing sanctuary and our magnificent pulpit, and I thought of what that woman had said: "After 9/11, my children all called and asked, 'What did St. Luke's do, and what did Jim say?'"

And as I let those words soak into my soul, I realized the sacredness of our responsibility as God's church. I realized how people in their joys and in their sorrows look to us, count on us, and depend on us for comfort and direction; how they look to us and count on us for strength, consolation, and encouragement; how they turn to us for insight and inspiration always, but especially in the tough times, the trying times of life.

The impact of that realization took my breath away, and I wanted to take off my shoes because I knew I was standing on holy ground. Like Moses standing before that burning bush years ago, I too came to grips with how overwhelming that call is, how important it is, how crucial it is, how awesome it is. And as I thought of that, I understood what Moses understood that day long ago—that our only hope, our only hope in performing our sacred responsibility, is that God is with us. Wherever we go, whatever we do, God will be with us. We can count on that.

That is God's great promise on page after page of the Bible—that God is with us as we stand on the holy ground of service, the holy ground of love, and the holy ground of sacred responsibility. So, we can in faith and trust say, "Here am I, Lord, send me!"

3

The Moments When We Say, "Ah"

Scripture: Philippians 4:10-13

*H*ave you ever wondered why people in the United States are so crazy about football? I think I figured that out some years ago at a high-school football game. There in a short period of two hours, the full spectrum of human emotions was played out. In that brief period of time, those of us who were there as interested and involved spectators experienced the gamut of feelings—joy and sorrow, agony and ecstasy, chills and thrills, ups and downs, "ahs" and "blahs." The team I was rooting for fell behind 13-0, and everybody on our side of the stadium felt so sad, so blue, so blah.

But then in the fourth quarter, our team rallied and scored two touchdowns and went ahead 14-13, with less than two minutes left in the game. We were deliriously happy. People were hugging and jumping and shouting and crying tears of joy. Our band was playing loudly, the cheerleaders were cheering, the pep squad was waving their pompoms, and the players were celebrating on the sideline with magnificent high-fives. It was an "ah" moment, a moment to relish, a moment to savor.

But four plays later, the other team completed a fifty-seven-yard pass play for a touchdown, and then they had the "ahs" and we had the "blahs." We sat in stunned, stony, sad silence as the final seconds ticked off the clock. So quickly our ecstasy had turned to agony; so quickly our victory had turned to defeat; so quickly our joy had turned to sorrow. I kept saying to myself, *It's just a ballgame*, and it was; and yet, in a way, it was something more—it was a microcosm of life. It was a strange and wonderful and confusing mix of some of our most powerful emotions.

Through that experience, I realized again what I already knew, namely, that life for all of us is a dramatic mixture of moods and feelings and happenings. Life is no smooth railroad trip across level plains; but rather it is more like a roller-coaster ride, with the "ahs" of the mountaintop and the "blahs" of the valley. We can all remember those high moments of joy when life feels good and really worth the living. However, we also know those low moments of depression and discouragement when we feel hopeless and we are ready to throw in the towel and give up on life. We have all experienced both the "ahs" and "blahs" of life. We can all relate to the words of the spiritual: "Sometimes I'm up, sometimes I'm down, oh, yes Lord."

Speaking of the ups and downs, and the ahs and blahs of life, remember the apostle Paul. If ever a human being had a life of mountains and valleys, joys and sorrows, challenges and threats, victories and tragedies, it was the apostle Paul. He reports in one of his letters that he had known the debilitating experiences of life and the abounding experiences, too. He had faced both plenty and hunger. He had known incredible triumphs, but he had also had troubles enough to dampen his spirit and break his soul. He so easily could have given in to the blahs.

The crowning blow came when he was arrested and sent to prison. Just when Paul wanted to take his ministry to Spain, he was thrown into jail. But from that prison cell, he wrote to his close friends at Philippi: "Now, don't worry about me. I have learned how to be content, no matter what the circumstances may be. I have learned the secret of contentment. I'm ready for anything, because Christ is my strength" (Philippians 4:10-13, paraphrased). In the experience and witness of Paul, we see a powerful axiom of faith—that God does not save us from trouble, but he does save us from defeat. God is with us in the ups and downs, the ahs and blahs of life.

How can we discover this contentment that Paul had, this contentment in all circumstances? How can we find this magnificent spirit of poise, grace, confidence, and strength that came to Paul through his faith in Christ? How do we handle the blahs when they come into our lives? What is the answer of faith?

First, Remember That It Is Temporary

Don't accept the blahs as permanent. Remember that "this too, will pass."

Fortunately, in some respects, our moods are as changeable as the weather. When my family first moved to Houston, someone told us, "If you don't like the weather here, just wait a minute; it'll change."

And that's the first thing to do in handling the blahs. Remember that it will pass; it will change. Momentarily, you may be under a cloud; but behind that cloud, the sun is still shining. And one day the cloud will move on, and you will be out in the clear again.

Second, Make High Use of Low Moments

Harry Emerson Fosdick put it like this:

> Don't waste sorrow, it is too precious. . . . trouble and grief can add a new dimension to life. . . . Quality of character never could have come from ease, comfort, and pleasantness alone. . . . No hardship, no hardihood; no fight, no fortitude; no suffering, no sympathy; no pain, no patience. . . . Don't misunderstand me. I'm not singing a hymn of praise to trouble. We all alike dread it, but it is inevitably here to be dealt with one way or another. An old adage says, "The same fire that melts the butter hardens the egg." Some people end in defeat and collapse . . . [but] others—thank God!—can say with Paul, "We triumph even in our troubles." (Harry Emerson Fosdick, *Dear Mr. Brown* [Harper & Row, 1961]; pages 182–83)

Low moments will come to all of us, to be sure, but we don't have to be defeated by them. We can rise to the occasion and turn our defeats into victories. We can make high use of low moments.

Remember the old Texas tale about a young cowboy (who looked like a strange combination of Don Knotts, Tim Conway, and Jim Carrey) who came bursting into a saloon one day, shouting, "Somebody painted my horse green, and I want to know who did it!" Just then, a huge fellow, 6 feet 10 inches tall, 280 pounds of bulging muscles, stood up to his full height and said in a gruff voice, "I did it! And what *of* it?" Quickly, the young cowboy rose to the occasion and responded, "Well, I just wanted you to know that the first coat is dry, and he is ready for the second coat!" That's what you call rising to the occasion!

We can do that, too. We don't have to let the low moments get us down. With the help of God and by the grace of God, we can use them, convert them, redeem them, learn from them, grow on them, and even turn them into breathtaking victories!

That's what Paul did. It was a low moment indeed when he was sent to prison. Talk about a "blah" moment! Paul could have resented that. He could have given in to bitterness and self-pity. He could have cursed the darkness and cried out, "Why did God let this happen to me? After all I did for him, where is God now?" He could have withdrawn and quit on life. Or, he could have accepted it stoically and said, "Oh well, I've done my part."

But no, Paul was a master at making high use of low moments. For there in that prison cell the apostle Paul sat down and wrote much of the New Testament. After twenty years of constant missionary wanderings, Paul had time on his hands—time to think and meditate and penetrate the deeper mysteries of the faith and time to write it all down. And that's just what he did. Yes, Paul made high use of low moments. With God's help, we can do that too!

How do you handle the blahs? First, remember that it is temporary; and second, make high use of low moments.

Third, Learn to See the "Ah" of Things

Sometimes we experience breathtaking moments in our life which are so powerful that words cannot describe them, we can only exclaim, "Ah!" in admiration. The high moments of "Ah!" are available to all of us. They are as near as breathing, all around us—if only we could open our eyes to see them, our ears to hear them, and our hands to touch them.

Many of these "ah" moments are very ordinary, day-to-day things. Recently I ran across a list of breathtaking "ah" moments that can be triggered by some very ordinary, everyday experiences:

35

1. The celebration of God's incredible creation, the seashore or the mountains, a beautiful sunrise or sunset
2. A tender love experience—that very special moment in life when you and another person become as one and, if only for a moment, become the whole world for one another
3. Childbirth—especially the sight of the first child (or grandchild)
4. Physical exercise, such as walking or swimming and, for some people, running, and for others, gardening
5. A religious experience—feeling the presence of God powerfully in your life
6. Art—especially religious art
7. Scientific discovery, such as solving a difficult math problem
8. Poetry or soul-stirring music
9. Creative work
10. Recollection and reflection
11. Beauty—encountering the beautiful

How did you do? Anything there that makes you exclaim, "Ah"? All of them touched me, with the possible exception of the math problem. Solving a math problem makes me say, "Whew!" rather than "Ah!"

In the Scriptures, we see that those who have the "ah" experiences are equipped to better handle the blahs when they come. Remember Moses at the burning bush? That was a breathtaking "ah" moment, and it served him well later when he surely must have faced the blahs as he tried to deal with a dangerous pharaoh and a difficult people.

Or what about Jacob? Remember how he cheated and connived; but then, in a dream, he saw a ladder leading to heaven. He encountered God, an "ah" experience, and he expressed it for all of us: "Surely the LORD is in this place— and I did not know it!" (Genesis 28:12, 16). I wonder how many times God has been in the place where we were and we didn't know it; we missed it; we didn't understand or perceive it. If it could happen to a renegade like Jacob, it could happen to us.

Our need is not so much to create the breathtaking "ah" experiences and situations, but to celebrate the ones that are all around us. This calls for sensitivity and openness that some of us may not have at this moment. One thing is for sure: We all need the eyes of faith! How easy it is to miss our high moment because we don't expect it, because we are blind to it or refuse to open our eyes. "God is in this place"—and we need to learn how to see him and feel him and know the "Ah!" of his presence. Nothing will help us to handle the blahs better than that.

Fourth, Attack the Blahs With a Positive Faith

Remember how Paul put it: "I can do it all." That's positive, isn't it? "I can do it all! I'm ready for anything through Christ, who lives in me and strengthens me" (Philippians 4:13, paraphrase). In one of her poems, Ella Wheeler Wilcox describes how ships on the ocean go in different directions by setting their sails to take them where they want to go. They don't just drift with whatever wind happens to come by. They purposefully and intentionally set their sails to choose their own course. In like manner, she indicates that in our voyage through life that we have the power with the help of God to choose our own course, to set our own sails, or as she puts it, " 'Tis the will of the soul / That decides its goal" (*Leaves of Gold* [The Coslett Publishing Company, 1965]; page 137).

There's a great lesson here. It's not so much what happens to us, but how we respond inwardly that counts. Our calling and our challenge is to attack the blahs with a positive faith.

37

Fifth, Remember That There Is an Outside Source of Strength

This is the good news of our faith, and this is the most breathtaking realization of all. This was the key to Paul's contentment, strength, poise, and confidence. He knew that whatever happened, God was with him, and nothing, not even death, could separate him from God's love. This is why he could say, "I'm ready for anything, for Christ is my strength." When you feel that, it makes all the difference.

When we were living in Houston, a member of our church shared with me a poem that her grandmother had written many years ago. It has meant a lot to me over the years. It depicts two farmers having a dialogue; one asks the questions, the other answers. It has these powerful words:

> 'What you gonna do when the river overflows?'
> 'Sit on the gallery and watch her go.'
> 'What you gonna do if ya hogs all drown?'
> 'Wish I'd lived on higher ground.'
> 'What you gonna do if ya cow float away?'
> 'Throw in after her a bale of hay.'
> 'What you gonna do when ya cabin leaves?'
> 'Climb up on the roof and straddle the eaves.'
> 'What you gonna do when it comes on night?'
> 'Trust in God and hold on tight.'
> 'What you gonna do when your strength gives way?'
> 'Say, "Howdy, Lord, it's judgment day."'

I love that illustration because it reminds us that God does not save us from trouble, but he does save us from defeat. We can be ready for anything, for Christ is our strength and our salvation.

And when we know that with confidence, then it so much easier to see and seize and celebrate the breathtaking "ah" moments of life. They are all around if we have the eyes to see them, the ears to hear them, the hearts to feel them, and the faith to embrace them as God's special gifts.

4

THE MOMENTS WHEN GOD MEETS US WITH HIS LOVINGKINDNESS AT EVERY CORNER

Scripture: Psalm 139:7-12

*H*er name is Paige. She is five years old. She is my good friend. I see her at church most every Sunday morning.

One evening a few years ago, Paige was watching television with her mom and dad. Suddenly, a newsflash showed President George Bush walking to a meeting. The President was surrounded by a group of men in dark suits. Paige asked her parents, "Who are those men with the President? Why are they with him?" Her parents answered, "They are members of the Secret Service. They go with the President everywhere he goes. They travel with him always. They protect him and take care of him and keep him safe at all times." And Paige replied, "That's what Jesus does for me!"

That was a breathtaking moment for her parents, and for me when her parents shared that experience with me. Paige was right, wasn't she? This is the great promise of Jesus in the Scriptures: "Lo, I am with you always" (Matthew 28:20, NKJV). In other words, Jesus is saying,

"You can count on me. Come what may in this life and in the next, I will be with you to watch over you and take care of you and keep you safe." And the assurance of that takes our breath away.

Some years ago, a dedicated journalist was exhausted. He was at the breaking point. He was physically tired, emotionally drained, under severe nervous strain, confused, perplexed, stressed out, not knowing which way to turn concerning some highly important decisions he had to make.

He was staying at a friend's home prior to speaking at a big meeting. His friend said to him, "My friend, you look tired. Would you like to escape all this chatter and rest in a room upstairs?" The journalist said that he would like that very much.

To his delight, he was led to a beautiful, peaceful room. A fire was burning in the fireplace, an easy chair was drawn up near to it, and at his elbow was a little table with a Bible on it.

The Bible was open to Psalm 59, and in the margin opposite verse 10, someone had written in pencil a fascinating interpretation that kindled his mind and warmed his heart (as it does my own). In the King James Version, the first portion of Psalm 59:10 reads like this: "The God of my mercy shall prevent me." Let me hurry to say that in old English, the word *prevent* means "to go before." So the verse means, "The God of my mercy goes before me." But the interpretation penciled into the margin read like this: "My God in His lovingkindness shall meet me at every corner."

The journalist said that when he read those words, the message came to him as light in a dark place, light from the very heart of God. It lifted him, consoled him, encouraged him, revitalized him, and gave him the strength and courage to make his decisions and to do what had to be done. It was, for him, a moment that took his breath away.

"My God in his lovingkindness shall meet me at every corner." That is our faith, our hope, our confidence. That is the overriding theme of the Bible.

And that is what the message in the Scripture for this chapter is all about—God in his lovingkindness meeting us at every corner. Read these magnificent words in Psalm 139:

> Whither shall I go from thy Spirit?
>   Or, whither shall I flee from thy presence?
> If I ascend to heaven, thou art there!
>   If I make my bed in Sheol, thou art there!
> If I take the wings of the morning
>   and dwell in the uttermost parts of the sea,
> even there thy hand shall lead me,
>   and thy right hand shall hold me.
> If I say, "Let only darkness cover me,
>   and the light about me be night,"
> even the darkness is not dark to thee,
>   the night is as bright as day;
>   for darkness is as light with thee. (verses 7-12, RSV)

Powerful words! Incredible words that represent one of the highest peaks in all of the Bible.

Recently, I received a letter from one of our church members. In it, she had a line that sums this all up. She wrote, "There is no spot where God is not." This is indeed what the psalmist is saying, isn't it? No matter what kind of trouble or heartache or darkness we have to pass through, God is there! There is no spot where God is not! God meets us at every corner with breathtaking lovingkindness.

Now, let's bring this closer to home and be more specific.

41

First, at "the Dropping-off Place, "
God Is There for Us!

That phrase in Psalm 139, "the uttermost parts of the sea," means "the dropping-off place." Remember that back in the psalmist's days, people believed the world was flat and that if you got to that totally remote place in the sea, you would drop off the face of the earth. We all know about "the dropping-off place," don't we? When we feel rejected or deserted or ridiculed, when our hearts are broken and our hopes are dashed, that's when we know firsthand the pain of "the dropping-off place."

Some years ago, a Roman Catholic priest was taken into captivity by terrorists in the Middle East; and he spent many horrible months as their prisoner. After his release, he told of the awful abuse and the inhumane treatment that he and others had endured. He had spent his life helping needy people and that's precisely what he was doing that day, when suddenly armed men came and captured him. They kept him in solitary confinement for weeks and weeks. One day, the captors tied explosives all over his body; and the priest was certain this was the end for him. Another day, the captors attached a chain to the ceiling of the priest's cell; and he was certain they were going to hang him. But these tactics were all designed to torture and intimidate him.

The priest told of how one day he was bound and trussed like a turkey, and shoved into a rack beneath a flatbed truck, where the spare tire is usually stored. Apparently his captors were taking him to a new hideout. But the priest felt certain that they were taking him out to kill him.

As he took that awful ride, he remembers what gave him the courage to face that moment. He kept saying these words to himself: *I am a human being of worth and dignity. I belong to God. I am redeemed. I am a child of God. He cares for me.* And over and over, he said the powerful words, "Nothing can separate me from the love of God in Christ Jesus our Lord; and nothing can separate me from him and his love" (Romans 8:38-39, paraphrased).

Then, the priest prayed over and over these familiar words: "Yea, though I walk through the valley of the shadow of death, I will fear no evil: for thou art with me" (Psalm 23:4, KJV). Again and again, he spoke aloud the strong words of Jesus, "Lo, I am with you always." Later, he said, those promises of God to be with us in every circumstance kept him alive and sane and hopeful.

Now, it is very unlikely that any of us will ever have to go through that kind of traumatic experience, that kind of blatant abuse; but we all know what "the dropping-off place" feels like and how painful it is. But when it comes, when it happens, when we feel cast out to the uttermost parts of the sea, to the dropping-off place, the good news is that God will be there for us, even there with his special brand of love, grace, encouragement, and acceptance.

So, that's number one: When you feel pushed by life to the dropping-off place, remember that God loves and accepts you, and that God will always be there for you. God in his lovingkindness will be there to meet us at every corner, even at the dropping-off places of life. I have found this to be so true in my own personal life. When I have had to walk through the valley of grief, every time, God was there for me. God was there for me at our dropping-off place, nearer than breathing and in ways that took my breath away!

Second, at the Place of Darkness, at the Place of Trouble, God Is There for Us Also

In the last week of November 1990, our daughter, Jodi, became extremely ill. She was nauseated, dehydrated, and

43

bent double with abdominal pain. The doctor took one look at her and put her in the hospital. All day Monday and Tuesday they ran tests, but no luck. The doctors could not pinpoint the problem. Meanwhile, Jodi was hurting more and more, and getting weaker and weaker.

Finally, on Tuesday night, she was rushed to the operating room for emergency exploratory surgery. The surgeon discovered that Jodi's appendix had ruptured. Their skilled hands, our fervent prayers, and God's healing power combined to produce a successful surgery and an excellent recovery; and in a matter of weeks, Jodi was back to teaching school and completely well.

Just before we got the word that our daughter was sick, we had a hundred things on our minds—so many things to do, so much to deal with and accomplish. Christmas was coming, there were year-end details, a conference meeting, sermons to write, other meetings to prepare for—hundreds of things to do—and then the call came: Jodi is really sick and facing exploratory surgery! Suddenly, all those things on our minds didn't seem important anymore. All that mattered was to get to our daughter, to be with our daughter in her time of trouble.

That's who parents are. That's what parents do. They love to be with their children anytime, but they especially want to be with their children when their children are in trouble. Jesus told us that God is like that. That's what the classic poem, "Footprints," is about.

In this much-beloved poem, a man describes a dream he has had in which he was walking along a beautiful beach with God. As they walk along, they see scenes from his life flashing across the sky and the man notices that in most of the scenes there are two sets of footprints in the sand; but he is also disappointed to see that during the hardest, toughest, saddest, most trying moments of his life that there is only one set of footprints. This is upsetting to the man and in frustration he tells God that he doesn't understand how God could leave him alone in the most difficult times of his life. He points out to God that in those scenes depicting his most troublesome times that there is only one set of footprints. How could this be? How could God desert him in those hard times when he needed God most? God responds by telling the man that he loves him and would never leave him and the reason there is only one set of footprints during those times of trouble was because those were the moments when God was carrying the man.

We can count on it. The Bible makes it clear: God will always be there for us, even at the uttermost parts of the sea, at the dropping-off place. God will also always be with us at the place of darkness, in the valleys and shadows and trouble spots of life.

Third and Finally, at the Place of Death, God Will Be There, Even There, Especially There

The word *Sheol* is a difficult one to translate. It means "the pit" or "the place of death."

Yesterday I drove by a beautiful cemetery, and I noticed again how people decorate the graves of their loved ones with flowers. Why do we do that? Have you ever wondered about that? Well, it's a beautiful Christian gesture. The flowers are symbols of new life and resurrection and the good news of our faith, that nothing (not even death) can separate us from God and his love.

That's precisely what the psalmist is talking about in Psalm 139:7-12. "If I make my bed in Sheol, if I just fall down and die, God will be there for me too, even at the place of death" (RSV, paraphrased).

45

Some years ago, a great Christian minister was devastated by the sudden death of his seven-year-old son. The staggering blow left him in the depths of despair.

One day while out for a walk, he came to a beautiful estate. He saw a little girl, about five or six years old, come running out through an iron gate. She closed the gate behind her.

Suddenly, the girl realized that she had locked herself out. She began to cry and beat on the gate hysterically. Quickly, her mother came running to the little girl. She opened the gate, took the little girl in her arms, carried her back inside, and comforted her, saying, "Everything is all right, honey. You know I wouldn't leave you out here all alone. You know how much I love you. You knew I would come, didn't you?"

As the minister saw that young mother coming to rescue her daughter, he remembered that God is like that—that no matter what the situation is, even at the place of death, God is there for us. The minister said, "In that moment, I saw with my spirit that there was love behind my shut gate also."

This is the hope, the confidence, the blessed assurance the psalmist is underscoring for us: At the dropping-off place, at the place of darkness, and even at the place of death, God is there for us, meeting us with breathtaking lovingkindness at every corner. Because there is no spot where God is not!

5

THE MOMENTS WHEN WE MOVE FORWARD, TRUSTING GOD

Scripture: Genesis 19:24-26; Philippians 3:13-14

*W*hen I was in the tenth grade in high school, I was a sprinter on the Memphis Tech High School track team. Back then, tenth grade was the first year of high school, so I was a real rookie on the track team. I had been running the 100-yard dash. I was also running on the sprint relay teams. In addition, I was doing the long jump and the high jump.

One day in a practice track meet, the coach suddenly decided to try me in the 220-yard dash. I had never run this event, so the coach called me aside to get me ready to run the race. He told me that he had noticed in the sprint relay events that I was running "the curve" well, and so he thought I would do well in the 220. "In fact," he said, "I am expecting you to win this event." He said, "Now Jim, listen to me. This is a 'full-speed-all-the-way-race,' so focus on getting a good start, and then run as fast as you can until you complete the race." Well, as it turned out, there weren't any superstar sprinters in the race that day, so I did end up winning the event.

The next day, the coach called me into his office and he said, "Jim, I am proud of the way you ran yesterday in the 220, and I'm going to let you continue to represent us in that race. But you made one terrible mistake that I don't ever want to see you do again. You almost lost the race because of it."

"What was that, Coach?" I asked. I honestly didn't know what he was talking about.

The coach said, "In the last twenty yards, you did it twice! You looked back over your shoulder twice, and you broke stride and stumbled, and the second place runner almost overtook you." And then he said, "Let me show you something." The coach dimmed the lights and flipped on a sixteen-millimeter motion-picture projector (we didn't have video in those days), and he showed me the last twenty yards of the race in slow motion—forward and backwards, backwards and forward, over and over and over again. He made me sit there and watch what I had done, and he was right. I had looked back over my shoulder twice, and my glance back, my look backwards, had thrown me off stride and almost cost us the race.

The coach had me sit there and watch that over and over, in slow motion and then in super-slow motion, and finally, he said, "Jim, the *good* news is that you were ahead. The *bad* news is you looked back, and it cost you. So the lesson is obvious: Don't you look back over your shoulder ever again. You keep your eyes focused straight ahead on the finish line!" And then, for emphasis, he added, "If you ever do that again, I'm gonna put horse blinders on you! Do you understand me, young man?" And I said what any high-school boy in his right mind would say in that moment: "Yes sir."

Now, that experience is something of a parable for us. Over the years, I have remembered that lesson many times.

"Don't look back, go forward. Focus on what's ahead, not on what's behind!"

That is precisely what the apostle Paul was saying in his letter to the Philippians. He put it like this: "Forgetting what lies behind and straining forward to what lies ahead, I press on toward the goal for the prize of the upward call of God in Christ Jesus" (Philippians 3:13-14, RSV). Paul loved athletics, and he often used sports illustrations (especially from track and boxing) in his writings. Here in Philippians 3, he is using this powerful track illustration to make his point: You can't rest on your laurels. You can't dwell on your past successes or your past failures. You can't run well if you are always looking back. Just focus on Christ. As hymn-writer Helen H. Lemmel put it, "Turn your eyes upon Jesus" (*The United Methodist Hymnal* [The United Methodist Publishing House, 1989]; page 349). Let that be your goal, and run toward him.

This is also the dramatic point in the Old Testament story of Lot's wife. She was told, "Don't look back at your old life. Look ahead. Move forward to your new life with God." But, she couldn't resist. She looked back, and "she became a pillar of salt" (Genesis 19:26).

I know people today who, if they really thought about it, could relate strongly to Lot's wife, because they spend so much of their time and effort and energy looking back that they become immobilized. They become like a pillar of salt, frozen in place, unable to move forward, just stuck in that spot because they are constantly looking back over their shoulders. They can't break away from the past, so they miss the joy of new life with God.

This message must be very important, because we find it dramatically underscored in both the Old and the New Testament of our Bible. Throughout the pages of Scripture, we find this lesson: Don't look back; remember Lot's wife. Don't look back; remember Paul's words. Don't look back; remember Christ's call. Don't look back; move forward toward new life with God in Jesus Christ.

Now, let me bring this closer to home with three thoughts.

First of All, Move Forward; Don't Look Back on Your Past Successes

That's a strange thing to say, isn't it? Don't look back on your successes; forget about your past accomplishments.

But the truth is that success does ruin some people. They do nothing but rest on their laurels. They "bask in the glow" of their past victories so much that they become spoiled and lazy and complacent, and they forget their mission, they forget their calling, they forget their priorities, and like Lot's wife, they become immobilized. They stop running forward, and they just become spiritually and emotionally paralyzed.

Last winter I heard a basketball coach in the postgame interview, after his team had lost a game in the closing seconds. His team had been ten points ahead with three minutes left, and they stopped hustling. They thought, *We can relax now. We've got it won. We've played so well.* And resting on their laurels, they lost the game.

The coach was not happy, and he said, "We couldn't stand success out there tonight. We got ahead and got cocky! We got a good lead, and then we just quit. For most of the game we played well, but we didn't finish it. We lost our concentration; we lost our intensity; we became lackadaisical and sloppy; we lost our focus; we abandoned our game plan. Our early success ruined us, and once again we did it: We snatched defeat from the jaws of victory."

50

You know what that coach was saying, don't you? He was saying, "We looked back on our past successes, and we turned into a pillar of salt." That's a pretty good parable for life, isn't it? Our own successes can do us in if we aren't careful. Our own successes can make us lazy and spoiled and complacent if we dwell on our past accomplishments and forget to give our best energies to the present.

Picture this. You are out at Minute Maid Park. The Astros are playing the Cardinals in a crucial game. The score is tied in the bottom of the ninth. The bases are loaded, and Craig Biggio (the former Astro) comes up to bat. The crowd is clapping and stomping and screaming for a hit to win the game. How do you think the crowd would feel if Craig Biggio called for a microphone and said to the Astros' fans, "Remember, now—I have already gotten three hits tonight. I have done my part, so don't expect too much now"?

First of all, Craig Biggio would never do that, because he has the heart of a champion. But if he did, how would the crowd feel? They wouldn't care at all about his earlier success at the plate. They want him to deliver now. They want him to come through now. They want him to drive in the winning run now. They are not even thinking about his earlier hits. And you know what? Craig Biggio would not be thinking about them either. He would step up to the plate, focused, determined, trying with all his might to get the game-winning hit, because he is a great athlete, a great person, a great gift to the game.

I don't know a lot about boxing, but I do know enough to understand two phrases that fight analysts use, phrases that carry over into other dimensions of life. I recently heard George Foreman commenting on television about an upcoming fight, and he used these two phrases. He predicted that one fighter (who had been very successful as a boxer) would lose, because, he said (here is the first phrase), "He has become a fat cat," and he predicted that the other boxer would win because, he said (now, here is the second phrase), "He is a hungry fighter."

Although I'm not an expert on boxing, I knew what he was talking about. "Fat cats" in any field are those who, because of their past successes, have become spoiled, lazy, complacent, self-satisfied, pompous, prideful, prima donnas; whereas those who are "hungry" are those in any field who are striving, stretching, struggling, working, dreaming, reaching, sacrificing, willing to pay the price.

As I thought of this, my mind darted back to one of the Beatitudes of Jesus: "Blessed are those who hunger and thirst for righteousness" (Matthew 5:6). And I also thought back to Paul's words to the Philippians: "Forgetting what lies behind, I press on."

The point is clear: As individual Christians and as a church, we have to constantly guard against the temptation to become "fat cats." We have to stay hungry!

We cannot relax on our press clippings.

We must not rest on our laurels.

We dare not dwell on our past accomplishments.

No wonder Paul resolved to forget his earlier achievements. He knew that there was a new challenge, a new opportunity in the present. And he calls upon us to forget what lies behind and to press on into the future and not look back on our past successes.

Second, Move Forward; Don't Look Back on Your Past Hurts

We need to forget and move on beyond those past hurts that dampen our spirits, drain away our energies, and poison our souls.

Dr. Paul Tournier, in his book entitled *A Doctor's Casebook in the Light of the Bible* (Harper & Row, 1976), tells of treating a woman for anemia. He had been working with her for months without much success. He had tried all kinds of medicines. He had tried vitamins and diet and exercise, but all to no avail. There was no improvement in the patient at all. As a last resort, the doctor decided to put her in the hospital.

However, as the woman was checking in, the hospital staff rather routinely checked her blood, and they discovered that it was fine. The woman was well, with no sign of anemia. Dr. Tournier checked her with the same results. Miraculously, she was healed. Intrigued by this, Dr. Tournier asked the woman if anything unusual had happened in her life in the last few days since he had last seen her. She responded by telling him that something out of the ordinary had indeed happened, that she had forgiven someone against whom she had borne a nasty grudge for a long time. They had reconciled. They were friends again and the woman was so relieved that she felt like she could at long last feel good about life.

You see, the woman's past hurt and her seething about it and her agonizing over it had made her ill. When she forgave the person who hurt her, when that reconciliation came, it was a breathtaking moment. The impact was so great, so powerful, that it literally and dramatically changed the physical state of her blood and made her well.

Wow! What a message is wrapped up in that story! What a crucial lesson for life is found here!

Don't let your past hurts immobilize you!

Don't let your past hurts fester within you!

Don't let your past hurts make you sick or "turn you into a pillar of salt"!

Go fix that! Go get reconciled. The apostle Paul is saying, "Forget about your hurts. Don't nurse grievances! Don't give in to self-pity! Put them behind you and go on with life!"

Move forward. Don't look back on your past successes or on your past hurts.

Third and Finally, Move Forward; Don't Look Back on Your Past Failures

Remember how Frank Sinatra used to sing those words: "Pick yourself up, dust yourself off, start all over again"? That's a nice song and a good thought, but the truth is, we need help with that. We can't really do that by ourselves. God is the One who can pick us up and dust us off and give us a new start.

That's why Jesus Christ came into the world. He came to give us forgiveness, a new chance, a new start, a new beginning, and to close the door on our past sins and failures.

His name was Christopher. He was nine years old. He was an orphan. Christopher had spent his whole life moving from orphanages to foster homes, and back again to orphanages. And then one day a wonderful Christian family came and adopted him. Suddenly, Christopher found himself in the loving embrace of this terrific family. Now, he had a mom, a dad, and three sisters who loved him and wanted him.

Christopher was happy, but he was worried sick. He couldn't believe that he belonged in this beautiful home with this gracious and loving family. If he did the slightest thing wrong, such as spilling his milk or letting the dog in or tracking dirt into the house as little boys will do, he would become hysterical and cry: "You're going to send me back to the orphanage! I *know* you will! I *know* you will! Please don't send me back!"

54

His parents would say, "Christopher, Christopher! You are not going back. This is your home! You are our son! We are your parents. We love you so much. You belong here with us." But Christopher just could not believe it. It felt too good to be true. He was just so afraid he might be sent back.

Finally, one night, that family did a beautiful thing. After dinner, the whole family went together into the living room for a very special ceremony. They let Christopher change his name. They asked him what new name he would like. He looked over at his three new sisters. Their names were Jeralyn, Jana, and Johanna. So, that night, Christopher became Jay. That was his new name, and that was the beginning of the turnaround in this young man's life.

At last, he felt like he belonged, because of the Christlike grace and love and compassion of his new family. He stopped looking back over his shoulder and moved forward to become a new person in Christ; and today Jay is all grown up, and he is as fine a Christian gentleman as you would ever want to meet.

The point is clear: Focus forward, lean forward, move forward. Don't look back. Forget your past successes, your past hurts, and your past failures; and press on toward God and the awesome, breathtaking moments that God has in store for you.

6

THE MOMENTS WHEN GOD GIVES US THE STRENGTH TO RISE ABOVE BITTERNESS

Scripture: Matthew 5:38-42

*I*t was a Friday night. We were sitting in a football stadium doing what we had done many times before: watching our son, Jeff, play football. He was playing the best game of his high-school career when suddenly, trouble struck; and so quickly, a pleasant evening at the football game turned into an awful nightmare. Jeff was down, writhing in pain, holding his right knee. Through the field-glasses, we could see his face; he was in anguish, and so were we.

Only moments before, he had been so happy. He had scored a touchdown on a fifty-yard pass play. Then came this critical moment, third down and fifteen yards to go in a crucial drive. Jeff was playing wide receiver. He cut across the middle. The pass was thrown high and behind him. I didn't think he had a chance to catch it, but somehow he went up high, twisted back, and came down with the ball. Just as his right leg was planted stiff on the ground, the hit came, head-on at the knee.

Immediately, everyone in the stands knew from the jarring collision that both players were hurt. The safety man for the other team was knocked out momentarily, and Jeff had torn ligaments in his right knee. He had made the catch and had held on to the ball, despite the severe injury. It was a first down, and Jeff's team went on to score and win. A few days later, Jeff's teammates would tease him about giving his body for the team.

He was carried off the field in excruciating pain, and placed in the back of a pickup truck where we tried (without much success) to keep his leg stable as we were rushed across the practice field to a waiting van, and then on to the clinic and eventually to surgery. The surgery was successful, and over time, Jeff recovered nicely. But it was a slow, arduous, difficult, agonizing process.

Extensive surgery, followed by several days of intense pain in the hospital, six weeks in a heavy cast, three months on crutches, and weeks and weeks and weeks of physical therapy. When something like that happens, so many "if only's" flood into your mind: If only the pass hadn't thrown Jeff off-balance; if only his right foot had been an inch off the ground when he got hit; if only the tackle had been a fraction higher, it never would have happened. But it did happen, and Jeff was compelled to live with that fact. He was compelled to deal with that difficult situation. He was compelled to face that adversity. He didn't want to be out for the rest of the season. He didn't want to be incapacitated for months. He didn't want to miss the whole basketball season. He didn't want to be unable to drive a car for six months. He did not want to be in that position, but he was compelled to be.

Now, when something like that is thrust upon us unwanted and we are compelled to face it, we have a choice: We can either become bitter and cynical, or with the help of God, we can rise above it, learn from it, grow on it, and witness through it.

Jesus gives a powerful illustration of this in the Sermon on the Mount when he says, "Go the second mile." Remember how he put it in Matthew 5:41, "If anyone compels you to go one mile, go with him two miles" (NKJV, paraphrased). The key word here is *compel*. To understand this, we have to go back in history and get into the shoes of these people of first-century Palestine.

They were living in an occupied country. They were, at the time, a slave state to Rome. Roman soldiers were all about, with their flashy uniforms, swaggering attitudes, and sharp spears. At any moment, with no advance notice these Roman soldiers could "compel" any citizen of the occupied country to supply food, to run errands, or to carry baggage; and sometimes the soldiers exercised this right of compulsion in the most cruel, tyrannical, and unsympathetic ways.

There was no let-up. Always, this threat of "being compelled" to do something hung over the people of Palestine. At any moment, a Jew might feel the touch of the flat of a Roman spear on his shoulder and know that he was compelled to do what he didn't really want to do—compelled to respond and serve the Romans, sometimes in the most menial, thankless, degrading, and trying ways. This is precisely what happened to Simon of Cyrene when he was compelled to carry the cross of Jesus toward the hill of Golgotha (Matthew 27:32). They jerked him out of the crowd and made him do it. Simon had no choice; he was required by the law of that day to do it.

Now, that is the background of this difficult teaching of Jesus, and I imagine that Jesus' hearers that day found this "second-mile teaching" hard to swallow and difficult to accept. But the fact is that Jesus is underscoring here a tremendously important lesson—namely, don't give in to bitterness; don't give in to resentment; don't give in to hatred;

don't feel that you have to strike back or retaliate; don't let the actions of others control or determine your attitude. Rather, in every circumstance, rise above it and respond with love and courage, serenity and confidence. Don't fall down; rather, stand tall. Don't wallow in self-pity. Don't give in to hostility; rather, live always in the discerning, breathtaking spirit of love and peace.

Now, obviously we don't have to worry about Roman soldiers suddenly appearing to make us do things we don't want to do. But we all do live under the constant threat of compulsion. That is, at any moment, without warning, life can compel us to face some problem, some challenge, some adversity that we would much rather do without. This is a relevant teaching for all of us, because when life compels us to deal with a difficult situation, we need to know how to go the second mile and then some.

Let me break this down a bit and show you what I think it means for us today.

First, Going the Second Mile Means to Overcome Evil With Good

That is, do something positive, see the problem as an opportunity, take the offensive. If people are ugly to you, you don't have to be ugly back. Don't burn them up; instead, melt them down. Don't descend to their level, but overcome evil with good. J. Wallace Hamilton tells an interesting story about this in his book *The Thunder of Bare Feet* (Fleming H. Revell Company, 1960). He tells of a sheepman in Indiana who was troubled by his neighbors' dogs killing his sheep. "Sheepmen," he writes, "usually counter that problem with lawsuits or barbed-wire fences or even shotguns, but this man went to work on his neighbors with a better idea. To every neighbor's child, he gave a lamb or two as pets; and in due time, when all his neighbors had their own small flocks, they began to tie up their dogs, and that brought an end to the problem" (pages 141–42).

So it goes all through the New Testament: "Do not be overcome with evil, but overcome evil with good" (Romans 12:21). That is at least part of what it means to go the second mile.

Second, Going the Second Mile Means Always Doing More Than Is Expected

There are always three possible ways of doing things, and we have to choose between them. Let me get you to try these on for size and see if you find yourself, or someone you know, somewhere between the lines.

One approach is to do the absolute minimum, and not a stroke more—just enough to get by. We can do it in such a way as to make it abundantly clear that we hate the whole thing, and that even though we are doing it, we are seething inside with resentment and hostility. That's the first approach, and sadly, that's the way some people choose to do most everything.

A second approach is to tackle our task, whatever it may be, with a smile, with a gracious courtesy, with an extra effort, and with an unflinching determination not only to do this thing, but to do it well and joyously. That's a good approach.

But there is a third way that is even better, and I think it is the most Christian of all; and that is to do everything we do as if we were doing it for God himself, as if God himself were our employer. That's what it means to go the second mile, to always do more than is expected, to do whatever we do—from washing the dishes to teaching our children—as if there were a touch of the sacred in these tasks; to do everything we do as if we were doing it for God himself, as if God himself were our employer.

The magnificent prayer of Saint Francis is breathtaking in its beauty, and it is a marvelous expression of this approach:

> Lord, make me an instrument of Thy peace.
> Where there is hatred, let me sow love;
> Where there is injury, pardon;
> Where there is doubt, faith;
> Where there is despair, hope;
> Where there is darkness, light;
> Where there is sadness, joy.
> O Divine Master, grant that I may not so much seek
> To be consoled as to console;
> To be understood as to understand;
> To be loved as to love;
> For it is in giving, that we receive;
> It is in pardoning, that we are pardoned;
> It is in dying, that we are born to eternal life.

"Going the second mile"; what's that all about? What is Jesus teaching us here? He is showing us how to overcome evil with good, how to always do more than is expected.

Third, Going the Second Mile Means Taking Responsibility for Your Own Attitudes

We are hearing a lot these days about the problem of "codependency." As I understand it, that means some people become so dependent on others for their self-worth, their being, their validity, that they actually let other people determine what they do, how they feel, and how they act. Their "self-starter" won't work. Like a billiard ball, they go through life just bouncing off of others, without the slightest understanding that they have the power within themselves to determine their own destiny. If other people around them are happy, then they feel that they have permission to be happy. If other people around them are unhappy, then they feel obligated to be unhappy too. They operate as thermometers rather than as thermostats. They let other people determine their attitudes.

Now, when Jesus says, "Go the second mile," what he means is this: You are a child of God. You are a human being of integrity and worth, and you do not have to be dependent on the actions of others for your feelings of self-worth. When that Roman soldier comes into your life, you don't have to let him dictate your attitudes or rain on your parade. When that troublesome situation suddenly explodes into your life, you have a choice—you can either let it get you down, or you can, with the help of God, rise above it.

A few years ago, a minister friend went to serve a church in Texas. He was forty-two years old at the time but he looked twenty-two. The first week there, a woman came into the church office, saw the minister, but she did not know who he was and she said to him, "Hey young man, I have some clothes in the trunk of my car for the neighborhood center. Go get them and bring them in and I will give you a dollar." With a smile and without saying a word, the minister went out and after several trips got the clothes into the church office. Then the woman said, "Find someplace to store them and then take them over to the neighborhood center when it opens. Here's your dollar." "No need to pay me," the minister said, "I'm glad to help out. Why don't you just put the dollar in the offering plate on Sunday morning?" The following Sunday morning the woman came to church and realized that the young man she had been ordering around a few days before was her new senior minister. She was so embarrassed and after the service, she started to apologize, but he interrupted her and said, "There is no need to apologize. I am always glad to help a friend." From that moment that woman became one of the church's most loyal and generous supporters.

Let me share one more thought.

Finally, Going the Second Mile Means to Live Daily in the Spirit of Christ

Over the years in speaking and writing, I have used a large number of inspirational stories to clarify the particular point I am trying to make at the moment. I have a number of favorites. The following story is one of my all-time favorites.

One wintry morning in Birmingham, a little boy who had no shoes was standing on a grating outside a bakery trying to warm his feet. It was cold and snowing slightly. A woman came along and when she saw that little boy shivering in the frigid air, her heart went out to him. She couldn't stand it. She went over to him and asked why he was bare-footed on such a cold morning... and where was his coat. He said he had no shoes or coat. The woman took him by the hand, led him to a department store where she bought him some new shoes, several pairs of socks and a warm winter coat. When they came out of the store, the little boy was so excited that he immediately ran off down the sidewalk... headed for home to show his family his new presents. But then, suddenly, he screeched to a stop, turned around and came back to the woman and said, "I forgot to thank you!" Then he said, "Could I ask you a question?" "Certainly," said the woman, "Ask me anything." Then he asked,

"Are you God's wife?" The woman was embarrassed at first; but then she said, "No, I'm not God's wife, but I am one of his children."

And the little boy said, "I knew it, I knew it. I knew you were some kin to him!" That was a breathtaking moment for that woman

Let me ask you: Can people tell by the way you live that you are kin to God? Can people tell by the way you act, the way you speak, and the way you respond to adversity that you are kin to God? Can they see the Spirit of Christ in you? It's something to think about, isn't it?

When God reaches out to touch our hearts as only God can and gives us the strength to rise above bitterness, hostility, and resentment, it takes our breath away!

7

THE MOMENTS WHEN FAITH OVERCOMES DOUBT

Scripture: John 20:24-31

*I*n *Through the Looking-Glass*, the White Queen told Alice that she was over one hundred years old. Alice said that she just couldn't believe that. "Can't you?" asked the Queen. "Try again: draw a long breath, and shut your eyes" (*Alice's Adventures in Wonderland & Through the Looking-Glass*, by Lewis Carroll [Signet Classics, 2000]; page 176).

Now, that's the way some people come to the Christian faith. They want to believe—desperately they want to; but like Alice, they find it hard, and they wonder, they question, they brood, and they doubt.

There is some comfort in knowing that one of the first disciples was a "doubter." Everybody knows his name, "Doubting Thomas." *Sesame Street* has its Oscar the Grouch; Snow White and the Seven Dwarfs have their Grumpy; Charlie Brown and the *Peanuts* kids have their Lucy. And the early disciples have their "Doubting Thomas."

As we might expect, it is Thomas who is the last of the disciples to believe the Resurrection, and then, only after dramatic proof. When the risen Lord first appeared to his followers, one man was missing: skeptical Thomas. Can't you see him walking gloomily through the dark streets of Jerusalem, sadly thinking back over what had happened. *I should have known this wouldn't work. It was all too idealistic. It was all too good to be true. And now, this incredible rumor, this women's talk of resurrection. What do they know? I was there. I saw it with my own eyes. It was a ghastly sight, this crucifixion business. I saw the nails in his hands; I saw the spear in his side; I heard the Master cry out. I'll never believe again. I've seen what this world does to goodness. These are hard times, tough times. It's over now. Dead people don't rise, not when Romans kill them.*

Can't you just see Thomas moping through the darkness alone, not wanting to face the others, brooding in solitude, tears streaming down his cheeks, wanting to be left alone, a bit like a wounded dog that crawls under the house to suffer and die out of sight? Then, when the other disciples come to tell him that they have seen the Lord and have talked with him, Thomas just can't believe it. He wants to believe, but deep down in his cynical nature, he just can't accept it. He is sure that they have been dreaming or hallucinating or something. "Impossible," he says to them. And then he blurts out those words that have stayed with him over all these years: "Unless I see in his hands the print of the nails . . . and place my hand in his side, I will not believe" (John 20:25, RSV).

"Doubting Thomas." He is an interesting character, isn't he? Can you identify with him? I guess we all can to varying degrees of intensity. I guess there is some of "Doubting Thomas" in all of us. Like Thomas, we all have our moments of despair and skepticism. "Doubting Thomas"—Easter has "good news" even for him, even for the somber pessimist.

We are going to get to that in a moment, but before we do, I want us to look at a rather basic question, namely this:

What is it that produces a doubter? Run that through your computer, and see what you come out with. What produces a doubter? What causes people to be "Doubting Thomases"? Think about it. What would you put on your list?

Here are some ideas I put down: Some doubt because they are dropouts. Some doubt because they choose to be negative. Some doubt because they mistakenly assume that the only truth is scientific truth. Some doubt because they are afraid to make a leap of faith.

Let's take a look at each of these.

First, Some Are Doubters Because They Are Dropouts

They drop out on the church. They quit. They detach themselves from the fellowship of believers, and as a result, malignant tentacles of doubt creep in and take over. Where faith was once supported by the church's community of love and hope and belief and commitment, now the support is gone, the props are knocked out, and somber pessimism and cynicism rule the day.

Look at Thomas. Christ came to the disciples, to the church community, that night in the upper room. He startled them, surprised them, renewed them, resurrected them. But Thomas missed out, simply because he was not there. Thomas missed it, because he was absent.

What about us? How many great moments of revelation have we missed out on because we weren't there in church? Ministers love this part of the story. When we want to dramatize and underscore the importance of church attendance, the importance of the church fellowship, the significance of being involved in the church, we like to point to Thomas and say, "Look at that: Look at what Thomas missed because he had dropped out. He missed the miracle. He missed the moment. He missed the risen Christ because he wasn't there, because he had dropped out of the group, because he had detached himself from the fellowship of believers."

Why do people doubt? Many reasons, of course, but often it is simply that they have dropped out of the church. They are living in a moral fog, a state of confusion and uncertainty, because they have cut themselves off from the community of Christians and what our forefathers and mothers called the means of grace.

Some years ago, I heard Dr. Pierce Harris speak. At the time he was pastor of the First Methodist Church in Atlanta, Georgia. He served that great church in a signal way for twenty-five years and was one of the most popular preachers in America. On the day I heard him preach, he told about being invited to preach in a maximum-security prison in Georgia. On that occasion, he said, he was introduced in an unusual way by one of the prisoners.

The prisoner stood up in front of his fellow inmates and said, "It is such a privilege for me to introduce to you our noted speaker, Dr. Pierce Harris, and to do this I want to tell you a true story.

"Several years ago, two boys lived in the same community in North Georgia and attended the same school, played with the same bunch of fellows, and went to the same church and Sunday school. One of them dropped out of church because he felt that he had outgrown it and that it was 'sissy stuff.' The other boy kept going because he felt that it really meant something in his life. The boy who dropped out is Yours Truly, the prisoner making this introduction today. The boy who kept going to church and Sunday school is the famous preacher who will preach to us this morning."

Now, let me say something to you with all the feeling I have in my heart: Don't drop out; don't lose your church;

70

don't cut yourself off from the roots of faith. If you are in church, please stay there. If you have dropped out or slipped away, please come on back. Or, if you have never gotten in the church, there's no better time than now. We want you and welcome you with open arms. But more than that, God wants you and welcomes you with open arms.

That's the first thought I put down. Some are doubters because they have dropped out of the church. Here is a second thought.

Second, Some Are Doubters Because They Choose to Be Negative

I know a woman who sees everything negatively. Quite often, doubt is a matter of disposition. It is an emotional way of looking at life. It is choosing to be negative rather than positive.

J. Wallace Hamilton, in his book *What About Tomorrow?* (Fleming H. Revell Company, 1972), makes a fascinating contrast of the two key disciples Simon Peter and Thomas:

> We can easily imagine Peter and Thomas getting on each other's nerves. Peter by nature could agree quickly and believe easily, but Thomas must lag behind to investigate and question. Peter loved the limelight; Thomas lingered in the shadows. Peter saw the doughnut; Thomas was always looking at the hole. When Peter had dark thoughts, he doubted them; Thomas was suspicious even of his hopes. (pages 60–61)

Belief or unbelief, doubt or faith, positive responses or negative reactions; it is our choice to make. While it is true sometimes that we may get deceived because we believed too much, far more often we get cheated because we believe too little.

One afternoon, two strangers, a small boy and an older man, were fishing from the banks of the Mississippi River.

As time passed they discovered that, although the fishing was rather poor, their conversation was quite good. They talked about many things and became good friends.

Toward the end of the day, they saw a large riverboat moving slowly in the distance. Excitedly, the young boy began to shout and whistle and wave his arms. The older man watched him for a bit and then said, "Son, you can make all the noise you want to, but that boat is not about to stop for you." "Oh yes, it will," said the young boy confidently. "You just watch. I'm sure it will stop for me."

Suddenly the boat began to slow down. It turned and moved directly toward the little boy on the riverbank. When it arrived, the gangplank was lowered, and the little boy started on board. The older man scratched his head in amazement and, unable to contain his curiosity, he shouted, "How did you do that? How did you know that boat would stop for you?" "It was easy," said the young boy, "because, you see, my father is the captain of this boat."

Why did Thomas doubt? It was in part because of that negative streak he had been cultivating in his personality for a lifetime, but it was also because he didn't fully understand at the time that his Father God was in charge, that God was Captain of the boat.

Knowing that can make all the difference. Knowing that can give you confidence. Knowing that can convert a pessimist into an optimist. Knowing that can take your breath away!

Third, Some Doubt Because They Mistakenly Assume That the Only Truth Is Scientific Truth

The real truth is that the things we value most cannot be proved in a scientific laboratory. Scientific methods are valuable, to be sure; but they are not the only road to truth.

I have here a fascinating quotation. See if you can figure out who said this:

> We don't know the millionth part of one per cent about anything. We don't know what water is. We don't know what light is. We don't know what gravitation is. . . . We don't know what electricity is. We don't know what heat is. We don't know anything about magnetism. We have a lot of hypotheses about these things, but that is all. But we do not let our ignorance of these things deprive us of their use.

Who do you think said that? Interestingly, these are the powerful words of Thomas Edison (see *Dear Mr. Brown*; page 76).

In my opinion, some of the most important truths cannot be scientifically documented. The love of a woman for a man and a man for a woman; you can't put that under a microscope, but I believe it is real. The warmth a mother feels for her child; you can't examine it with a magnifying glass, but I believe it's real. Honesty, courage, patience, forgiveness, morality, love, faith, goodness, humility, grace, self-sacrifice; these can't be put in a test tube, yet they are among the things that matter most.

Please don't misunderstand me. I am not knocking scientific truth or the scientific method; I am all for it. All truth is God's truth. I am simply saying that there is a special brand of truth and reality that cannot be contained in a laboratory. Remember how Jesus put it to Thomas: "Have you believed because you have seen me? Blessed are those who have not seen and yet believe" (John 20:29).

That brings us to the final point, "the leap of faith."

Finally, Some Are Doubters Because They Are Afraid to Make a Personal Commitment

Their doubt is not so much doubt as it is the fear of making a big decision. If you want to learn how to swim, there is only one way to do it: You have to get into the water. You can read all kinds of books about swimming; you can watch good swimmers in action; you can stand on the side of the pool and go through the motions. But there is only one way to learn how to swim: You have to get into the water.

The same is true with faith. You have to dive in.

Back during World War II, a young paratrooper told about his first parachute jump. He said, "The first time I leaped out of a plane everything within me resisted. I had listened to lectures, I had mastered the techniques of using a parachute, I had practiced jumping under simulated conditions, but still I did not believe for sure that this frail piece of silk could actually hold me up." Then he said, "Nothing in this world compares with the thrill I experienced when I leaped into the sky, pulled the cord, and found that the whole thing was actually true, that the parachute would support me and take me safely to the ground."

Now, if you apply that experience to religion, you have what the great theologians have called "the leap of faith." There comes a point when we simply trust God and leap out in faith. We will never discover the truth of Christianity until we make a leap of faith, until we live and act out its truth and stake our very lives on its power to support us. In my opinion, the biggest obstacle for us is not some thorny theological problem, but rather our hesitancy to make a decision about Jesus Christ, our hesitancy to make a personal commitment to him and to his way of life.

Now, a quick footnote about the "good news" for the "Doubting Thomases" of the world. First, bless Thomas's heart, because he wanted the firsthand experience. That's a "feather in his cap." We need a little of that in us, because we live in a "spectator world": We want to watch others perform; we want to be entertained. Thomas, though, couldn't be content with being a spectator. He wanted to be on the playing field. He wanted the firsthand experience. He wanted to touch it, feel it, be a part of it. And that's great; we could all use some of that.

Second, also notice that Christ came to him, saw his frailty, saw his weakness, and still loved him. Christ understood Thomas's need and met it, and enabled Thomas to make his "leap of faith."

That's the good news of the Christian faith. Christ comes to us like that, with understanding, with compassion, with forgiveness, with new life, with resurrection. He comes to bring us out of the tombs of doubt, into the new life of faith. And when we experience that breathtaking moment, then we can say in faith with Thomas, "My Lord and my God!"

THE MOMENTS WHEN GOD REDEEMS OUR TROUBLES

Scripture: Psalm 23

On Monday, August 29, 2005, Hurricane Katrina slammed with devastating and amazing force into the Gulf Coast just east of New Orleans, Louisiana. With screaming, shrieking, 175-mile-per-hour winds, Katrina smashed ashore and destroyed houses and buildings; turned over cars, trucks, and boats; swamped Mississippi's beachfront; blew out windows in hospitals, hotels, and high-rises in Alabama, Louisiana, and Mississippi; submerged entire neighborhoods up to their rooftops in flood water; separated families and loved ones; claimed numerous lives; and left thousands and thousands of people homeless.

The dramatic images of Hurricane Katrina are still vivid in our minds: mind-boggling devastation along the Gulf Coast; unforgettable, heartbreaking flooding in New Orleans; people on rooftops, holding on for their lives and being air-lifted by helicopters to safety; people by the thousands standing outside of the Superdome in New Orleans, watching and waiting for buses to arrive; people filing by corpses to get onto those buses to bring them to Houston (and other destinations); thousands of survivors lying on cots in the Astrodome in Houston, with volunteers flocking there from all over the city to help them with food, water, clothing, support, medical aid, and encouragement.

I will never forget the picture of a woman falling on her knees in front of the New Orleans Superdome, and crying, "Please, help us!" Or survivors walking through the Astrodome, holding up signs looking for their loved ones. Or the man in the yellow jersey who had tried desperately to hold his wife and three children above the floodwaters, describing through tears how his wife was swept away from them.

And I remember that couple who, in the rush and the confusion of the evacuation out of New Orleans, had gotten separated from their newborn baby, and the tearful, joyful reunion when their baby was found alive and well in a Fort Worth hospital.

And I recall the elderly man in Biloxi who rode out the storm in his boat. His boat ended up on land, and the man sat there in the boat for four days until his son came and found him. The son said about his father, "He is something! He has survived the Great Depression, World War II, the Korean War, two terms in Vietnam, a number of storms, and now Katrina. My dad is a survivor, that's who he is!" The father said, "I don't look for trouble. It just seems to come and find me."

I was out at the Astrodome in Houston the day after Katrina hit, and I met a handsome young couple that told me they had walked out of the flood in shoulder-high water. They were okay, but they desperately were looking everywhere for her mother.

I also visited with an older man who was sitting on his cot on the floor of the Astrodome. He had arrived from New Orleans at 3:00 A.M. that morning. I said to him, "Welcome to

Houston. I am sorry for all you have been through. I'm glad you are safely here, and we want to help you. How are you doing this morning?" I was touched by the man's answer. It took my breath away. He said, "I'm blessed. I have lost everything, but I'm still here. I have food to eat and water to drink. I have air-conditioning and a bathroom. I have a cot and a blanket and a roof over my head. Yes," he said with a tired smile, "I am blessed! Thank you, thank you and the people of Houston; but most of all, thank God!"

Hurricane Katrina will go down in history as one of our nation's worst catastrophes; and it reminds us of a universal truth, namely this: Every single one of us, at one time or another, will have to face trouble. Not one of us is immune from the storms of life.

There is no wall high enough to shut out trouble.

There is no life, no matter how much it may be sheltered, that can escape from it.

There is no trick, however clever, by which we can evade it.

Sometime, somewhere, maybe when we least expect it, trouble will rear its head and confront and challenge every one of us. The psalmist did not say, "I will *meet* no evil." He said, "I will *fear* no evil!" (Psalm 23:4, KJV). So, the question is not, Will trouble come to me? It will! Rather, the question is, How do I respond to the troubled waters of life? How do we as Christians deal with the problems, the burdens, the heartaches, the broken dreams?

A veteran minister was speaking one day to a class of theological students in a seminary. He said to them, "Never preach a sermon without some word of comfort for the troubled and sorrowing, because there will always be someone within the sound of your voice who has a heavy heart."

Well, what do we do when life tumbles in? How do we respond to the difficulties of life? Is there a bridge over troubled water? Surely Christianity has something to say about this, because the great symbol of our faith is a cross!

To get deeper into this, let me suggest three breathtaking things to remember when we have to face trouble.

First of All, Remember That God Is With Us

That is the great promise of the Bible: God will always be with us, in every circumstance of life, and indeed, even beyond this life. Come what may, the one thing we can always count on is that God will be with us, giving us the strength we need; and when we feel God's presence with us in those dark and difficult moments, it takes our breath away.

One beautiful spring morning, a man in New York City took his son with him to walk around the streets of Manhattan. The streets were very crowded that day. The little boy started out holding on to his father's finger. However, after being pushed and jostled and bumped by the crowd, the little boy grew tired and he said, "Please, Dad, take hold of my hand now; I can't hold on much longer."

Sometimes that's what we have to do. We entrust our troubles to God and ask him to hold us up and get us through.

Some years ago, some friends of ours in another state wanted me to perform their daughter's wedding on a Saturday night. They said, "We know you don't like to be away from your church on Sunday morning, so if you will come, we will get a private plane to take you back to Houston right after the wedding."

After the reception, they took me out to the airport to board the private plane. As I boarded the plane, I was surprised to see the bride and groom seated there. I thought, *Oh my goodness, I have done the wedding, and now I'm going on the honeymoon!* But the pilot said, "We're going to drop the bride and groom off at Love Field in Dallas. You can sit back here with them or up front with me, whichever you would like." I chose the co-pilot's seat to let the bride and groom have their post-wedding privacy.

We flew quickly to Dallas, where I said "good-bye and best wishes" to the newly married couple. Then, just as the pilot taxied out for our take-off to Houston, it suddenly started to rain. Then it began to storm. The wind was howling and blowing fiercely. Thunder was rumbling. Lightning was flashing. Golf ball-sized hail started falling. The air traffic controller told us that DFW Airport had just been closed, and we had better take off in a hurry if we were going, because there were now tornado warnings being issued.

We took off. Wind shear turned the plane sideways three times as we were taking off—over and back and over, but I wasn't scared. Now, I flinched a bit when the plane was flipping sideways, but I wasn't really frightened and for three reasons.

First, I trusted the pilot. It was out of my hands, so I had to trust him. Sometimes we have to just trust God to pilot us through the storm.

Second, from my co-pilot seat I could see the weather radar screen, and I could tell that in about one minute we were going to fly right out of the storm into clear skies.

Third, I trusted God. I knew God was with us. I knew that come what may, God would be with us, because the Scriptures tell us that nothing can separate us from the love of God in Christ Jesus our Lord (Romans 8:38-39).

That's the first and the most important thing to remember when we are hit by the storms of life: God is with us, and we can trust him. So, we simply go forward doing our best and trusting God for the rest.

Hymn-writer Edward Hopper expressed it like this: "Jesus Savior, pilot me / Over life's tempestuous sea; / Unknown waves before me roll, / Hiding rock and treacherous shoal. / Chart and compass came from thee; / Jesus, Savior, pilot me" ("Jesus, Savior, Pilot Me," *UM Hymnal*; page 509).

That's number one: Remember that God is with us.

Second, Remember That God Can Redeem Our Troubles

This is the good news of our faith—that God can redeem, that God can take bad things and turn them into good things, and that moments of redemption like this do indeed take our breath away.

That is also our calling as Christians, isn't it, to work with God to turn defeats into victories? We see many examples of this in biography.

Edison failed as a newspaper salesman, and consequently he turned to scientific research.

Lincoln was disappointed in his law career. He considered himself a failure at the age of forty-six and thus turned in the direction that led to the White House.

Whistler wanted to be a soldier, but he flunked out of West Point and then turned to art.

Redeeming our troubles—using them—this is a key to Christian living, learning by the grace of God to triumph even in our troubles. Now, sometimes this takes creativity.

Five-year-old Donnie was being brought up in a very conservative home with a rigid observance of the Sabbath. "No playing on Sunday!" That was the rigid rule. But one Sunday, Donnie's mother caught him sailing his toy boat in the bathtub.

"Donnie," she cried, "Don't you know that it's wicked to sail boats on Sunday?"

"It's all right, Mom," replied Donnie. "This isn't a pleasure trip; this is a missionary boat on its way to Africa!" Now, *that's* what you call rising to the occasion!

In a deeper sense, that's what we can do with the help of God. When trouble rears its head, by the grace of God we can rise to the occasion and creatively use our trouble for good.

Jesus was a master at this. He didn't endure or resent the conflicts he had with the Pharisees. He didn't just put up with them or tolerate them. He used these conflicts productively, creatively, redemptively.

Remember the day when a man stepped up in the crowd and broke in on Jesus' teaching and tried to trip him up with loaded questions? It was a difficult, tricky, troublesome situation; but look what Jesus did. He told the parable of the good Samaritan (see Matthew 22:34-40; Mark 12:28-34; Luke 10:25-37). And remember the cross? Jesus used it and made of it God's victorious messenger.

So, when we have to face troubled waters in this world, first we can remember that God is with us; and second, we can remember that God can redeem our troubles.

Third and Finally, Remember That God Can Use Us to Help Others Who Are in Trouble

Our church worked closely with the American Red Cross from the beginning of the Hurricane Katrina crisis, so much so that when you went to the Astrodome to work as a disaster volunteer and the police officers saw your St. Luke's nametag, they waved you right in. The Red Cross asked our church to oversee all the donations of food and clothing being brought to Reliant Park. What a thrill it was to see people coming from all over the city to bring clothes and food, water and diapers, and formula and toys to help the survivors of Hurricane Katrina. When a disaster like this strikes, there will be a few people who will try to take advantage of the situation for their own selfish gain; but most people (by far, most people) will reach out with love and compassion and generosity.

Where did they learn that? Where did they learn to be loving and caring like that? Well, most of them learned that from their church. Most of them learned it from Jesus.

In the immediate aftermath of Katrina, I attended a meeting of pastors and church and community leaders who were trying to figure out creative ways to help the Katrina survivors. In that meeting, I heard a story that touched my heart.

A noted minister dreamed that he had died and appeared before Saint Peter at the entrance to heaven. Proudly he told Saint Peter his name and said with confidence, "I served as a very successful minister for over forty years. I'm sure you will find my name prominently displayed in the Book of Life." Saint Peter looked through the *Ministers* category; and then he shook his head, "No. I can't find your name here anywhere."

The minister said, "Oh, *I* know: It's probably listed under *Scholars*. I did write fourteen books." Saint Peter looked under *Scholars*, but again, no luck. The man's name was not there.

The minister was getting a bit rattled now, and he said, "Look under *Builders of Mega-Churches*: I'm sure that's where my name will be." And once again, Saint Peter looked, but to no avail. The man's name was not there.

The minister was heartsick as he turned to walk away, but just then an angel said, "Wait a minute. I think I recognize you. I knew you looked familiar, but now I know why. Aren't you the one who fed the sparrows every morning?"

"Well, yes," the minister said. "After breakfast, I did always go out and spread the leftover bread crumbs in the back yard for the sparrows."

With that, Saint Peter said, "Well, come on in, Reverend, the Lord of the Sparrows wants to thank you. The One whose eye is on the sparrow wants to welcome you to heaven."

When we reach the gates of heaven, I don't think we will be asked about our accomplishments. I think we will be asked if we cared for our neighbors and helped those in need in the Spirit of Jesus Christ.

When it comes to trouble, there are three breathtaking things to remember. Remember that God is always with us. Remember that God can redeem our troubles. And remember that God can use us to help others who are in trouble.

9

THE MOMENTS OF RESPONSIVE GRATITUDE

Scripture: Luke 19:1-10

*H*ave you heard the story about the young woman minister who was assigned to be the pastor of a church in a small farming community? The people of that church had never had a woman pastor before, and they didn't quite know what to make of this. Many of them (to put it bluntly) were unhappy and suspicious.

But very soon, the young minister won them over. She had extraordinary abilities and a deep commitment. She was an outstanding preacher, a keen administrator, a natural-born leader, and a wonderful pastor; and in no time, she had won her way into the hearts of all the people in the congregation—all, that is, except for two crotchety old farmers, who were hard-nosed, closed-minded, and extremely set in their ways. They didn't like change of any kind, and they certainly didn't take to this newfangled idea of having a young woman as their preacher. The minister tried everything she could think of to get close to them, but to no avail. They were cool and grumpy and unbending toward her, in their crusty old ways.

Finally, someone in the congregation said to her, "Go fishing with them. They love to fish, and maybe if you can get out on the lake with them, they will get to know you better and accept you. That might just do the trick. That might just melt their hard, cold, cynical hearts. Try it; go fishing with them."

The young minister liked the idea; so after church the very next Sunday, she suggested it. She asked the two old farmers if she could go fishing with them sometime. They frowned and grunted and groaned a bit, but finally they relented: "We'll meet at the café at 5:30 Wednesday morning, and if you're late, we'll not wait on you one minute," they said to her. "Don't you worry!" she answered. "I'll be there!"

Wednesday morning came, and they went fishing. They drove to the lake, got into the boat, pushed out from the shore, and commenced fishing. The gruff old farmers were surprised to see that the young woman did exceptionally well. She not only caught the first fish, she caught the first *five* fish. All of them were prize catches; and each time she would pull one in, the two old farmers would frown and groan and mutter and complain under their breath.

Shortly, a crisp wind blew up. The young minister felt chilled a bit, but she didn't want to disturb the fishing of the two old farmers, so she said, "I'm feeling a little bit chilly, so if you will excuse me, I'll run up to the car and get my sweater." With that, she stepped out of the boat and, miraculously, walked right across the water toward the shore. As the grumpy old farmers watched her "walk on water," one turned to the other and said, "Well, would you look at that? Should've known it: She can't even *swim!*"

I have a sneaking suspicion that that probably is not a true story! However, it does make an interesting point, namely this: There are a lot of people in the world today just like those two old farmers, aren't there? Miracles everywhere, and yet they are unable to see them, unable to appreciate them, and unable to celebrate them. These people use all their energy being cynical and grumpy, looking for the negative, focusing on it intently and harping on it constantly, and, sadly, missing the moments that take our breath away!

Of course, the truth is that all of us have our moments of spiritual blindness, moments when we are just unable to see how blessed we are. The riches of life, the riches of God are all around us; and yet so often, we fail to see them because we tend to magnify our difficulties, overlook our advantages, and neglect to see the good in what we have. That's why we need the spirit of gratitude! This spirit of appreciation not only reminds us to give thanks to God for all that we have; but it also reminds us of who we are, to whom we belong, and upon whom we can depend.

There is a beautiful example of the real spirit of thanksgiving in the New Testament, in the story of Zacchaeus. In Jesus' breathtaking encounter with Zacchaeus, we discover a fascinating formula for responsive gratitude and how it can dramatically change our lives. Remember the story with me. Jesus and his disciples were going to Jerusalem. Jesus was heading toward the cross. As they came to Jericho, a great crowd gathered to see him.

Zacchaeus was in the crowd. The Scriptures tell us that he was "a chief tax collector and was rich," and that he was disliked and despised by the people of Jericho, for a number of reasons. For one thing, they disliked Zacchaeus because he was the chief tax collector. He was responsible for gathering the hated Roman tax on the products of Jericho, such as balsam, and the taxes upon the costly imports from Damascus and Arabia. In the day of Jesus, the tax collectors were known for their greed; and they were considered outcasts, classed with thieves and cutthroats. Zacchaeus was a chief tax collector, so he was greatly despised.

Also, the people of Jericho regarded Zacchaeus as a traitor. He was a fellow Jew who had betrayed his people, his nation, his faith, and his God. To them, he was a turncoat who had gotten rich at their expense; so they resented him and rejected him.

This was the setting when Jesus came to Jericho that day. Zacchaeus was also eager to see Jesus; but being a man who was not very tall, he could not see over the crowd. He ran ahead and climbed a sycamore tree in hopes of getting a glimpse of the great teacher. When Jesus saw Zacchaeus, Jesus sensed his loneliness; and Jesus' heart went out to him. Jesus went over to the tree and looked up and said, "Zacchaeus, hurry and come down; for I must stay at your house today" (Luke 19:5). It was a moment of amazing grace for Zacchaeus, a powerful, awesome moment that took his breath away. Why, of all the people in Jericho, Jesus had reached out to him!

Zacchaeus, overwhelmed by the Master's acceptance of him and by this special honor, jumped down quickly and welcomed Jesus—and Zacchaeus's whole life was changed! Zacchaeus was so grateful for this acceptance, so filled with thanksgiving that it absolutely turned his life around. Christ does that to us! Thankfulness does that to us.

Notice that Jesus gave him no material gifts. Jesus gave him something better: love, respect, and acceptance. Zacchaeus was so thankful, that his lifestyle was totally changed. Why, it even touched his pocketbook. "Look, half of my possessions, Lord, I will give to the poor; and if I have defrauded anyone of anything, I will pay back four times as much" (19:8).

You see, that's what real gratitude does. It takes our breath away, and it changes our lives.

Let me show you what I mean. Christ gave Zacchaeus three things: a new appreciation, a new evaluation, and a new motivation. Let's take a look at these special qualities, one at a time.

First, Christ Gave Zacchaeus a New Appreciation

Up to that point, Zacchaeus seems to have been basically selfish, thinking only of himself. His motto was, "What's in it for me?" But then Jesus came into his life, and that special love ignited within Zacchaeus the spark of gratitude.

You see, there is no such thing as an ungrateful Christian. Christianity is, by definition, thanksgiving. Why do we come to church? Because we are thankful. Why do we sing our hymns? Because we are thankful. Why do we serve God? Because we are thankful! Why do we love one another? Because we are thankful to God to be part of his family.

Now, most of us respond appreciatively to what is unusual or rare. For example, if somebody called us today and told us that we had just inherited twenty million dollars, chances are that we would be appreciative of that. If someone called today and told us that we had just won a Mercedes or a trip to Hawaii, we would probably be grateful for that. But please notice that it is Jesus' enthusiasm for the seemingly ordinary and commonplace things that reveals his real appreciative spirit.

Remember Jesus' frequent references to simple things—brooms, candles, leaven, old cloth, and the like. Such things we so easily take for granted; but Jesus saw in them the truths of God, the goodness of God, the blessings of God, and he wove them into the very texture of his message. Look also at his appreciation of nature—flowers, birds, seeds, sunsets, the wind, the grass of the field; all spoke to him of the Creator.

Not only that, but whoever so appreciated people? Now, most of us appreciate the great and famous personalities such as Schweitzer or Saint Francis or Mother Teresa or John Wesley or Paul or Moses. But Jesus saw every person, every single person (even a Zacchaeus), as a child of God; and he appreciated and respected all people as a part of the family. Such was the appreciative spirit of Jesus.

In a hated tax collector, Jesus saw a promising disciple. In the weak and vacillating Simon Peter, he saw a rock (Matthew 16:18). In a cup of cold water, he saw divine compassion. In a lily, the commonest of Palestinian flowers, he saw a glory greater than Solomon's (Matthew 6:28-29). In a sparrow, the commonest of birds, he saw the providence and care of God (Luke 12:6). In a grain of mustard seed (the smallest of seeds), he saw the kingdom of heaven (Matthew 17:20; Luke 17:6). And in the face of a little child, he saw the keys to the Kingdom (Matthew 18:1-5).

Zacchaeus caught the spark that day when Christ walked into his life—a new appreciation!

Second, Christ Gave Zacchaeus a New Evaluation, a New Set of Priorities, a New Way of Measuring What Is Really Valuable

I saw a recruiting ad recently that fascinated me. The ad shows a young man with a six-day growth of beard, his shirt is ripped and hanging open, a canteen on his belt, his pants rolled up above his knees, his shoes in his hands, wading across a swirling, muddy jungle river. The caption reads: "Tim was voted 'Most Likely to Succeed.' *Now* look at him."

Underneath, the recruiting copy continues: "It's too bad. Tim had it made. Personality, initiative, a college degree with honors. Success and the good life were his for the asking.

92

Now look at him. Backpacking across some jungle river, giving his life to a pre-literate people barely out of the Stone Age, painstakingly creating a written alphabet from a previously unrecorded babble of sounds, working night and day, translating the pages of the New Testament, exposing the senselessness of superstition and ignorance, relieving pain and introducing the possibility of health, building a bridge of love and understanding to a neglected people. And to think . . . Tim could have been a success."

Then the ad concluded by listing the name of a Bible translation company to contact if you were interested in "Tim's kind of success." The point is clear. Tim had a new evaluation, a Christlike evaluation, a Suffering Servant evaluation.

You see, Jesus' way of evaluating success turns our world upside down. Or maybe better put, he turns our world rightside up. Jesus shows us that a sense of meaning is more important than material wealth, that discipleship is better than dollars, that helping others is more fulfilling than "feathering our own nest." Zacchaeus caught the spark that day, and he came down out of that sycamore tree with a new appreciation and a new evaluation.

Third and Finally, Christ Gave Zacchaeus a New Motivation

Zacchaeus got converted from selfishness to self-giving. Zacchaeus was converted from "That belongs to me!" to "I belong to that!"

If gratitude is recognition of God's generosity, then Christian living is imitation of God's generosity. After the devastating disaster of Hurricane Katrina, there were so many newspaper, television, and radio stories about the people who had suffered incredible loss as a result of that dangerous and destructive storm. A little boy in Houston was so touched and so moved to compassion by the plight of the Katrina survivors that he wanted to help. So, he started going door to door in his neighborhood asking people for donations to help out. He was asked by someone how much he hoped to raise in his relief efforts. Without hesitation, he said, "One million dollars." The questioner then asked if he thought he could actually raise a million dollars all by himself. And the little boy said, "Oh, no sir, my little brother is helping me."

When Christ comes into our lives, we can't sit still; we have to take up his ministry of love. That becomes the new motivation! It's expressed powerfully in the New Testament. Listen closely to these words:

> Beloved, let us love one another; for love is of God, and he who loves is born of God and knows God. He who does not love does not know God; for God is love. . . . We love, because he first loved us. If any one says, "I love God," and hates his brother, he is a liar; for he who does not love his brother whom he has seen, cannot love God whom he has not seen. (1 John 4:7-8, 19-20, RSV)

The great Christian Saint Augustine expressed it strongly like this:

> Love is the only final distinction between the children of God and the children of evil.
> All may sign themselves with the sign of Christ's cross:
> All may answer Amen, and sing Alleluia:
> All may be baptized,
> All may come to church and line the walls of our places of meeting.
> But there is nothing to distinguish the children of God from the children of evil, except love.
> They that have love are born of God:
> They that have not love are not.

Christ walked into Zacchaeus' life that day in Jericho long ago and gave him a new appreciation, a new evaluation, and a new motivation. Now, let me tell you something: He wants to do that for us today! Right now! He has a breathtaking, life-changing moment like that which he wants to share with you and me.

10

THE MOMENTS WHEN THE HOLY SPIRIT USES US

Scripture: Acts 2:1-4

*I*t happened at vacation Bible school. The leaders asked all of the children to think about how the world could be a better place. They discussed that question for a few days and then they asked the children to complete this sentence: "My wish for the world would be..." As they always do, the children amazed us with their thoughtful and poignant responses. Here are some of their wishes:

- That my daddy could come home from Iraq and there would be no more wars.
- That people everywhere would be kind to each other.
- That there would be more love and no hate.
- That everybody would just get along. My brother and I don't always agree, but we try to get along. We are in the same family.
- That people would learn what the Bible teaches about love and then just do it.
- That people would talk more and fight less.
- That everybody would obey the Golden Rule and then we would all be better off.

- That everybody who has food would send some to those who don't.
- That people everywhere would be kind and loving like Jesus.

Out of the mouths of little children! Fervent wishes, confessions, confidences, concerns, praise, and thanks. As we read these, we can understand more clearly why Jesus said, "Unless you become like little children, you shall not enter the kingdom of heaven" (Matthew 18:3, author's paraphrase).

In a sense, this is what the day of Pentecost is all about. The disciples had to become like little children before they could receive the Holy Spirit. Only then could they take up the torch of Christ's ministry, because only then did they have power from on high.

Go back a few months before this first Pentecost. Remember how the disciples were back then—arrogant, selfish, jealous, haughty, uppity, conceited. Do you recall this? Jesus had set his face toward Jerusalem. He was thinking deep thoughts as they walked down that dusty road, thoughts about love and sacrifice and commitment, as he moved steadfastly toward the showdown awaiting him in the Holy City. This was serious business, now. He was heading toward the cross!

And what were the disciples doing? They were walking along behind him feuding, fussing, and fighting among themselves. Do you remember what they were squabbling about? It was about which one of them was the greatest! About which ones of them should get the best seats and the top spots and the most power in the new Kingdom! How presumptuous! Jesus was thinking about love and sacrifice and commitment, and all the while they were quarreling about politics and clout and position.

They were missing the whole point. Jesus had to go to the cross to get their attention. He had to come out of the tomb to give them their wake-up call! Then, they were all ears, and he said to them, "Here! I want you to take up this torch. I want you to take up this ministry of love. I want you to do it now. I want you to be the church. I want you to teach the world this message of love and sacrifice and commitment. Now I must leave and go to the Father, and you will be my witnesses to all the world."

"But Lord," they protested in humility now, "we can't do that! We don't have the strength. We don't have the know-how. We don't have the courage!" "Don't worry," the Master said to them. "I will send you a Helper. I will send you strength and power. I will send the Holy Spirit to be with you always." And with that, Jesus ascended into heaven. Like little children, the disciples went back to the security of the upper room to think this all through, to sort this all out, and to wait for the Holy Spirit to come.

Now, think about this—their Lord has gone, the task is squarely on their shoulders; they feel so inadequate and so scared, and now they sit and wait for this Holy Spirit to come. And if you will remember from your study of the Gospels, the disciples were not very good at waiting. On earlier occasions, when Jesus had told them to wait, they either in their impatience did the wrong thing, or in their apathy fell asleep. Now here they are, waiting, and I can imagine the conversation in the upper room going something like this. Simon Peter, impatient as all get-out and pacing nervously, says, "This waiting is driving me up the wall. How long do we have to wait around here, anyway? Why can't we get on with this, or just forget the whole thing?"

And Doubting Thomas says, "We don't know anything about this Holy Spirit. I've never seen any Holy Spirit. I mean, how do we know it really exists? I know we can trust our Lord, but maybe we misunderstood him. Maybe no Holy Spirit is coming after all."

Next, Andrew speaks: "I've always been a good helper, but I don't know how to be a good leader. I'm not sure I can. I'm not wired up that way. I could serve the Lord enthusiastically when he told me what to do, but now he's gone, and I don't know how to do this. I don't know what we are supposed to do."

Then John says, "Look! He told us to wait here. He told us he would send help. I think we can count on that; but I have to tell you, honestly, I do feel so alone without him, and I do feel so helpless and inadequate without him."

James speaks up: "We've been waiting here a pretty good while, and nothing has happened. Maybe Thomas is right; maybe it's over. Maybe we should just face that and accept that and give up and go on back to our former jobs."

But then Simon Peter speaks again: "No! We wait! He told us the Holy Spirit will come, and I believe him. With all my heart, I believe him!" Just at that moment, as Simon Peter spoke those words, they heard something, a strange sound way off in the distance, becoming louder and louder as it moved toward them, a sound like the rush of a mighty wind, and it blew on that place. Oh, my, did it blow on that place! And they were all filled with the Holy Spirit. And they received courage and confidence and strength and new life, and through the power and presence of the Holy Spirit, they became the church of the living God on that Pentecost day. Through the gift of the Holy Spirit, they were empowered to take up the preaching, teaching, healing, caring ministry of Jesus Christ.

In his book *Who's Coming to Dinner? Jesus Made Known in the Breaking of Bread* (Abingdon Press, 1992),

Bishop Robert Morgan tells a powerful story about a Dutch pastor and his family who, during the Second World War, got into big trouble with the Nazis. The Dutch pastor and his family had been hiding Jewish people in their home to keep them safe from Hitler's forces. They were eventually found out; and one night in the darkness, they heard the sound of heavy boots and the loud impatient knocking on the door.

They were arrested and loaded into a cattle car to be taken to one of the notorious death camps. All night long, the Dutch pastor and his family rode along in heartbreaking anguish, jostling against one another and against the other prisoners who were jammed into the train's cattle car. They were stripped of any form of dignity and absolutely terrified. They knew they were being taken to one of Hitler's extermination centers. But, which one? Would it be Auschwitz, Buchenwald, or Dachau?

Finally the long night ended, and the train stopped. The doors of the cattle car were opened, and light streamed into that tragic scene. They were marched out and were lined up beside the railroad tracks, resigned to unspeakable pain, as they knew they would be separated from each other and ultimately killed. But in the midst of their gloom, they discovered some amazingly good news, good news beyond belief. They discovered in the bright morning sunlight that they were not in a death camp at all, not in Germany at all. Rather, they were in Switzerland!

During the night, someone through personal daring had courageously tripped a switch and sent the train to Switzerland, and to freedom. And those now who came to them were not their captors at all, but rather their liberators. Morgan writes, "Instead of being marched to death, they were welcomed to life." It was a breathtaking moment of amazing grace, indescribable joy, and indescribable relief. In the midst of his joy and relief, the Dutch pastor said, "What do you do with such a gift?" (pages 145–46).

Something like that happened to the disciples at Pentecost. They were afraid, confused, unsure, overwhelmed; and then came this incredible gift, the gift of the Holy Spirit! It took their breath away and turned their lives around, and empowered by this amazing gift, they went out and turned the world upside down.

One of my favorite hymns is one I first learned as a camp song. It's called "Spirit of the Living God," and it has these poignant prayer words: "Melt me, mold me, fill me, use me. / Spirit of the living God, fall afresh on me" (*UM Hymnal*; 393). This is a great song for Pentecost, because it shows us precisely what the Holy Spirit does for us. He melts us, molds us, fills us, and uses us. Let me show you what I mean.

First, the Holy Spirit Melts Us

The Holy Spirit warms us and melts our cold, cold hearts. Recently, I ran across a parable that makes the point.

Once upon a time, there was a piece of iron that was very strong and very hard. Many attempts had been made to break it, but all had failed.

"I'll master it," said the axe, and his blows fell heavily upon the piece of iron; but every blow only made the axe's edge more blunt, until it finally ceased to strike and gave up in frustration.

"Leave it to me," said the saw, and it worked back and forth on the iron's surface until its jagged teeth were all worn and broken. Then in despair, the saw quit trying and fell to the side.

"Ah!" said the hammer, "I knew you two wouldn't succeed. I'll show you how to do this!" But at the first fierce blow, off flew its head; and the piece of iron remained just as before, proud and hard and unchanged.

"Shall I try?" asked the small, soft flame. "Forget it," everyone else said. "What can *you* do? You're too small, and you have no strength." But the small, soft flame curled around the piece of iron, embraced it, and never left it until the iron melted under its warm, irresistible influence.

There's a sermon there, somewhere. Perhaps it means that God's way is not the way of force, but of love. God's way is not to break hearts, but to melt them. Perhaps it means that that is our calling as Christians—to melt hearts under the irresistible warmth of God's gracious love.

First, the Holy Spirit melts us.

Second, the Holy Spirit Molds Us, It Changes Us, It Shapes Us, It Redeems Us

In the early part of the twentieth century, a loud, outspoken atheist in London challenged a Methodist preacher to a public debate. The preacher accepted the challenge with one condition—that the preacher would bring with him to the debate one hundred men and women who would be witnesses of the redeeming love of God and what that love can do to the human heart. They would show how God had changed their lives and turned their lives around.

The minister asked his atheist challenger to do the same thing, to bring a group of persons who had been similarly helped by the gospel of atheism. Well, the debate never happened. The preacher was there with his one hundred transformed persons, but the atheist never showed up. The proposed debate turned into a worship service as one by one, these Christians shared the good news of how, through the power of Jesus Christ and the presence of the Holy Spirit, God had melted their hearts and remolded their lives.

The Holy Spirit melts us, and it molds us.

Third, the Holy Spirit Fills Us

A writer once said that without question the strangest sporting event of them all is the demolition derby. In this crazy event, automobiles race around a track and intentionally crash into each other. The last car moving is declared the winner! The writer pointed out that when you watch a demolition derby, you discover that many parts on an automobile are not necessary to its moving. Doors, hoods, mirrors, and hubcaps litter the track as the derby progresses, and the cars still move. But one thing is essential: an engine. A car must have power. No power, no movement!

In a similar way, we discover in living the Christian life that though discipleship has many parts, many components, there is one essential: the Holy Spirit. The Holy Spirit melts us, molds us, fills us, and enables us to move.

Finally, the Holy Spirit Uses Us

Often credited to Erasmus, the famous Renaissance scholar, is a classic story that was designed to emphasize how important it is that we take up the torch of Christ's ministry with great commitment. In the story, Jesus returns to heaven after his time on earth. The angels gather around him to learn about what had happened during his days on earth. Jesus tells them of the miracles, his teachings, his death on the cross, and his resurrection.

When Jesus finishes his story, Michael, the archangel, asks Jesus, "But what happens now?" Jesus answers, "I have left behind eleven faithful disciples and a handful of men and women who have faithfully followed me. They will declare my message and express my love. These faithful people will build my church." "But," responds Michael, "What if these people fail? What then is your other plan?" And Jesus answers, "I have no other plan!" That is a breathtaking thought, isn't it?

Jesus is counting on you and me. But the good news is, we are not alone. The Holy Spirit is here to melt us, mold us, fill us, and use us.

11

THE MOMENTS WHEN WE TRULY CELEBRATE LIFE

Scripture: Psalm 118:19-24

*A*re you making every day count for something? Are you really living life to the fullest? Are you really celebrating life? Do you see each day as a special gift from God—exhilarating, exciting, packed with fresh, new possibilities, with unique opportunities? Or is life passing you by?

Sadly, it is a well-documented fact that many people today are indeed unhappy and unfulfilled in the present moment. They are so caught up in looking to another day, that they miss the joy and meaning of *this* day. To some, the good days are way back there in the past. Others long for better days off in the future. Still others are harried and frustrated and depleted by the pressure-packed "busy-ness" of hectic modern-day living. And all of these are missing real life! They are not really living. They are coping, surviving, "hanging in there," but not really celebrating life!

Well, be honest now: How is it with you? Are you really living, or is life passing you by?

Life is a wonderful gift and yet without question sometimes it is hard, trying, challenging, and difficult. Because of that, sometimes we give in to the blahs. We feel blue, bummed out, depressed, gloomy. And sometimes this "down and out feeling" comes without warning. A harsh word from our boss, a parking ticket, a dented fender on the car, a bill that is higher than we expected, a family misunderstanding, a broken lamp, a disappointment at work, the onset of a cold, a lost pet, a problem our child or grandchild is facing, a financial concern, the intense feeling that we have disappointed someone...or a real tragedy. All of these and more can cause us to feel gloomy and depressed. Modern medicine spends a lot of time, energy, and effort helping people to fight off the blahs; but even with all the effective help and resources available, still many people turn to alcohol to drown their sorrows or drugs to escape them. Recognizing that the blues will indeed come, there is a better solution. Walk outside, feel the sunshine, breathe in the fresh air, touch the grass, look into the faces of little children, take in the miracles of God's creation and remember that the One who put this amazing, miraculous world in place loves you unconditionally.

Savor that, celebrate that, bask in the glow of God's power and God's amazing grace; and as you are doing that remember Orville Kelly. In his book, *The Positive Principle Today* (Ballantine Books, 1996), writer Norman Vincent Peale recounts the story of Orville Kelly, a newspaperman from Iowa, who went to the hospital at the age of forty-three for an examination and was told he had terminal cancer. Of course, he was stunned by this devastating news, as was his wife, Wanda. After further hospital tests, the doctors told Orville Kelly that he had from six months to three years to live. Tension began to build up in the family, even though the four children had not been told what was wrong.

Friends avoided discussing the matter with Orville and Wanda, simply advising them, "Don't think about it," and then quickly changing the subject. Communication almost stopped. Wanda wanted to say something loving, positive, hopeful; and Orville wanted to reassure her. But they couldn't find the simple, honest words; so they remained silent. Orville Kelly was put on a program of chemotherapy, and the long drive to and from the hospital was a painful, silent journey.

Finally, one day Orville said, "Let's talk about it. . . . I'm going to die from cancer . . . but I'm not dead yet. So let's start enjoying life again" (page 170). Then Orville Kelly suggested they go home and have a big barbecue, invite their friends, tell the children about it, and start living again. He didn't want to waste any more time that way.

A short time later, a fresh, new, and exciting idea came to Orville Kelly; and he said, "Each day I will accept not as another day closer to death, but as another day of life. I accept each day as a gift from God to be appreciated, enjoyed, and lived to its fullest" (page 171). And he decided to form a new program called "M.T.C."—"Make Today Count"! After all, Orville said, "We are all 'terminal' in a sense" (page 170). He simply knew that his terminus had been more clearly determined. He chose to see every day as a special and gracious gift from God.

And that is precisely what he went on to do. And you ought to hear Orville Kelly's description of the mighty Mississippi on a misty morning; or his incredible word picture of a bluebird sitting on the fence of an Iowa farm; or his play-by-play description of looking down on Boston through scattered clouds as his plane rose up into the sunlight; or his tribute to the smile on his wife's beautiful face. Though sentenced to death by a terminal illness, Orville Kelly actually became more alive by making each day count.

Isn't this what the psalmist was trying to teach us when he said, "This is the day that the LORD has made; / let us rejoice and be glad in it" (Psalm 118:24)? These magnificent words from the Psalms have been used for centuries at the opening of lofty worship services as an appropriate call to worship, but they are so much more—they are also practical and dynamic words for daily living.

If you and I could say that at the beginning of each day and really mean it, it would change our lives: "This is the day that the Lord has made and given to me as a gracious gift; I will rejoice and be glad in it, and be thankful for it." Recently, I saw a bumper sticker that says it well: *Today is God's gift to us. That's why it's called "the present."* Today is God's day. He has given it to us, and we should see it as a special gift and make it count. To waste it or corrupt it is sinful and destructive.

Well, how are you doing? Are you really making every day count? Or is life passing you by? As we think this through, let me suggest some ways we can make every day count.

First, We Can Make Each Day Count by Saying, "Today, I Will Be Aware!"

"Today, I will be sensitive to what is happening around me; aware of what I am seeing, hearing, and feeling; sensitive to the wonders and challenges of God's world."

Out of the Watergate controversy some years ago, a new word came into popular usage. Remember it? The word was *stonewall*. Politically, it meant "to be unaware; to act like you've heard nothing, seen nothing, and know nothing."

In a sense, that's what many of us do each day—we stonewall! We shut the world out! So many different interest

110

groups, marketing experts, political philosophies, commercial products, and religious gurus scream at us and clamor after us and try to win our attention, our loyalty, our support, and our money. We are so pushed and pulled, so mesmerized, so inundated that we stonewall the world out and shut our senses down. Like zombies, like robots, many people move relentlessly through life, unfeeling, untouched, uninspired, and unaware.

A few years ago, I was browsing through a magazine when I came upon an article that changed my life. It had an "Awareness Test" that was very simple, but it jolted me powerfully. The Awareness Test had five simple questions about our five basic senses. Namely, it asked: What were the last five sounds you heard? What were the last five sights you saw? What were the last five surfaces you touched? What were the last five fragrances you smelled? What were the last five things you tasted?

I had to work hard at remembering those things. How about you? Could you answer those questions right now?

Isn't it something how we stonewall? We become so insensitive, so unaware of what's happening around us; we shut down our senses and wall out the world. After reading that article, I went out into the courtyard of our church and turned my senses up a notch; and even though I had walked through that courtyard every day and often several times a day, this time I saw and heard and smelled and touched things I hadn't really noticed in years: the delicate and elegant nature of a butterfly, the agility of a squirrel scrambling up a tree, the amazing grace of birds flying overhead, the incredible fragrance of flowers in bloom, the unique texture of a pine cone, the loving expression of a teacher playing with her class at recess, the delightfully contagious laughter of little children.

111

I sat down in the grass and took it all in, and it was wonderful. I remembered our text from the Psalms: "This is the day that the LORD has made; / let us rejoice and be glad in it"; and I realized with shame how rarely I had been doing that, and I asked God to forgive me and to help me to be more sensitive, more aware.

We all know of the physical blindness of Helen Keller, but spiritually she had 20/20 vision. Listen to her words: "I have walked with people whose eyes are full of light, but who see nothing in wood, sea, or sky, nothing in city streets, nothing in books. . . . It were better far to sail forever in the night of blindness, with sense and feeling and mind, than to be thus content with the mere act of seeing" (*The Five-Sensed World* [The Century Co., 1908]; pages 84–85).

A good prayer to start each day might well be, "Lord, make me aware today! Give me the eyes of faith!"

Second, We Can Make Each Day Count by Saying, "Today, I Will Do Something For Someone Else"

"I will not live today by the code of selfishness; I will not live today by the law of the jungle; I will strike a blow for love today." It's the best therapy in the world. It's the key to happiness—getting outside yourself and thinking about somebody else.

Have you heard the story about the man who knelt at an altar and prayed for a friend, "O Lord, help my friend. Help him, Lord, before it's too late. Touch him, Lord, touch him even if just with your finger." Then it was as if he heard the voice of God whispering back in his ear, "*You* touch him; you are my finger."

One of the ways we, as Christians, make each day count is by reaching out and touching other people in the spirit of

Christ. "Today, I will be aware. Today, I will do something good for someone else."

Finally, We Can Make Each Day Count by Saying, "Today, I Will Trust God for Tomorrow"

Sometimes we are frightened a bit by the future, nervous about the unknown, anxious about what lies ahead; but here is where the Christian faith is amazingly helpful because God's great promise to us is that he will always be with us. That we can count on and trust him. We may not know precisely what the future holds; but we can know that, come what may, God will be there for us. So, we do our best and trust God for the rest.

In my study, I have an interesting book. I love the title: *Why Jesus Never Had Ulcers* (Abingdon, 1986). The author, Robert M. Holmes, a United Methodist minister in Montana, points out that Jesus never had ulcers because he remembered his priorities, what was important! He remembered his calling to be truthful, to not worry about success. He remembered who was in charge. He remembered to do his best today, and to trust God for tomorrow and all the tomorrows of eternity.

That's what it's all about, isn't it? That's how to make each day count. "Today, I will be aware. Today, I will do something good for someone else. And today, I will trust God for tomorrow."

This is the day the Lord has made, let us rejoice and be glad in it.

12

THE MOMENTS WHEN WE REALIZE THAT GOD REALLY DOES LOVE US

Scripture: Deuteronomy 30:15-20

*I*t happened some years ago, but I remember it vividly, as if it happened yesterday. I was working late in my office at the church. Everyone else on the staff had gone for the day. I was at my desk when I felt the presence of another person. Looking up, I saw standing at the doorway a young woman who appeared to be in her early twenties; she was crying softly. She said, "Jim, you don't know me. We have never met, but I know who you are and I didn't know anywhere else to go. I'm not a member of this church, but I have attended here a few times. I know it's late in the day and you probably are anxious to go home and I apologize for just walking in like this, but I need desperately to tell someone my story and then ask you a question that's eating me up inside. Let me tell you what a terrible mess I have made of my life and then ask you one question."

I invited her in and through tears and heavy sighs, her story unfolded. She married at eighteen. The marriage lasted two years. Her husband deserted her, just left home one day without warning and never came back. She said she found out later that he had cleaned out their checking account and had run off with another woman.

Hurt, scared, and confused, for a time she wallowed in self-pity; but then she became so lonely and so disoriented that she took up a lifestyle that was totally opposite every moral value she had ever been taught, a lifestyle so sordid that she couldn't even look at me as she described it.

"I should have come here to the church for help," she lamented, "but I went the other direction." She paused for a moment, took a deep breath, and continued her story. During her "self-pity period" as she called it, her girlfriends at work became worried about her and they said, "We've got to get you out of this apartment. He is not coming back. You've got to start living again." The friends meant well, but instead of bringing her to the church, they took her to "happy hour" at the local clubs and bars. She went on to describe how at first, she went along, but she just sat quietly on the sidelines, not participating. Then she said, "It went downhill from there, way down hill." She paused for a moment trying to find the courage to go on with her story, and then she said, "I knew better. I came from a good home with good parents. I went to Sunday school and church; but I was so messed up. I just pushed all that aside, and I began going to the bars everyday after work to find a different man to take home for the night."

Again she paused, looked at the floor and started in again, confessing that she felt so ashamed, so sorry, so remorseful, so penitent. She was. I could see it in her face and hear it in her voice.

Earlier that evening, two men had gotten into a fight over her at the bar she frequented and it was the two-by-four that got her attention. She realized how wrong, how, irresponsible, how immoral, and indeed how dangerous her lifestyle had become and she wanted to change and get back to the values she had cherished since childhood. She had left the bar immediately in fear and was driving through the streets of the city totally ashamed and embarrassed at what she felt she had become. Just as she came to the street where our church is located, the large spotlights on the church's front lawn came on and lit up the church's beautiful steeple against the dark night sky and she was even more jolted by how her life had spiraled out of control. The reality check hit. It all caved in on her and she was filled with guilt and sadness and remorse. At that moment, she pulled into our church parking lot and came to my office and told me her story with deep penitence.

Then came the question, "How could God ever forgive me for what I've done?" she asked. I responded, "God already forgives you. The question is: Can you forgive yourself? Can you learn from this? Can you make a new start with life with God's help?" She still seemed unsure of God's forgiveness, so I said to her, "Let me ask you to do something. I want you to imagine that you are my daughter and that you just told me your story exactly as you told it before. As a father, I would have two choices: On the one hand, I could say, 'Get out of my sight; you have dishonored our family. You are a disgrace. I disown you! Get out!'

"Or, on the other hand, I could reach out to you and say, 'I am sorry that this has happened. I love you and I want to help you. Let me help you put this all behind you. Let me help you make a new start with your life.'"

I paused for a moment to let it all soak in, and then I said, "Which one of those do you think I would do?"

She replied, "I think you would do the second."

"Why do you think that?" I asked her.

117

"Because," she said, "even though I don't know you that well, I do know that you are a father, and that you love your children."

"Precisely," I said to her, "And if I am capable of that kind of love and forgiveness, how much more is God?"

There is a vital choice each and every one of us has to face every single day of our lives, namely this: Do we choose light or darkness?

The Christian faith is helpful to us here because the Christian faith teaches us that God, the Great Physician, loves us, cares for us, values us, and treasures us. So, because of God's love and grace and presence with us, we can choose to live. We can choose to live joyously, gratefully, abundantly, victoriously, and meaningfully.

This is precisely what Moses is saying to the Israelites (and indeed to us) in the powerful passage recorded in Deuteronomy 30. By God's grace and power, and with God's help, Moses has led the Israelites out of Egyptian slavery; he has led them through the wilderness, and now he has brought them to the brink of the Promised Land. Moses is old and weak and tired now, and he can't go on with them. So he gives his people their final instructions. He tells them that when they get into the Promised Land they will be tempted to chase after false gods, they will be tempted to forget about God and his love and his covenant and his commandments; and so Moses implores them not to choose a destructive way of living, but to remember God's love and to choose life with God!

If Moses were here today, that is precisely what he would say to us: "Remember God's love; remember God's promise to always be with us, come what may; remember God's power; and remember God's way. Don't be deluded by the latest fads or the newest temptations. Just choose life with God." Or to

118

coin college football Hall of Fame Coach Darrell Royal's famous phrase, "Dance with the one who brung ya."

Remember the flight attendant who asked a man, "Would you like dinner?" The man replied, "What are my choices?" And the flight attendant answered, "Yes or no!"

That's what Moses is saying here. "You have a choice to make. Do you say yes or no to God?" And then he pleads with his people, "Please say yes! Choose life with God. Because God loves you, choose life with God."

Now, let me bring this closer to home with three thoughts that emerge out of the Scriptures and our faith.

First of All, Because God Loves Us, We Can Choose to Live in Confidence

In one of the *Peanuts* comic strips, Linus goes to Lucy for five cents' worth of psychiatric advice to help him face up to his fears. Lucy tries to pinpoint his particular fear. "Are you afraid of responsibility? If you are then you have Hypengyophobia!"

"I don't think that's quite it," says Linus.

"How about cats" Lucy asks. "If you're afraid of cats, you have Ailurophobia."

"Well, sort of... but I'm not sure..." says Linus.

Exasperated, Lucy says, "Maybe you have Pantophobia ... the fear of everything."

"That's it!" says Linus (*The Gospel According to Peanuts*, by Robert L. Short [John Knox Press, 1965]; page 77).

Well, bless Linus's heart; but the truth is, we all have moments of fear and anxiety. Again, the Christian faith can help us here, because God's repeated message to us in the Bible is, "Fear not, I am with you, come what may, in this life and in the next life."

Did you know that there are 365 "fear nots" in the Bible? Isn't that great? That's one for every day of the year, and the point is clear: Because of God's love for us and presence with us always, we can choose to live in confidence.

Candler School of Theology at Emory University in Atlanta is named in honor of Bishop Warren Candler. It is said that when he was on his deathbed, Bishop Candler was asked if he was afraid of dying, and if he was afraid of crossing over the river of death. I love his answer. Bishop Candler said, "No, I'm not afraid at all, because my Father owns the land on both sides of the river." That is confidence in God.

Elizabeth, too, had that kind of confidence in God. I first met Elizabeth in 1984. She was twelve years old at the time, and already she was devoted to God, to our church, and to prayer. Elizabeth excelled in everything she did. She excelled at camp, at school, and later at Princeton and at law school. She excelled as a litigator for a prestigious law firm. She excelled as a wife, a daughter, a sister, a friend, and as a member of our church.

At the age of twenty-four, Elizabeth was diagnosed with cancer. She was actually undergoing chemotherapy at the time she took the bar exam. She was so sick that she had to get up and leave the exam room twice to throw up, and still she "aced" the exam.

Elizabeth died at age thirty-three, after an eight-and-a-half-year battle with cancer. She died as she chose to, at home in her husband's arms. Her husband, David, was holding her and praying when she breathed her last breath on this earth. He "prayed her into heaven." David told me that it was the most difficult moment of his life, and yet at the same time, one of the most inspiring moments of his life, because Elizabeth exhibited this incredible sense of peace and faith and courage and confidence as she crossed over the river to be with God on the other side.

Elizabeth's courage came from her family, and especially from her mother, Ethel, who is without question one of the most courageous persons I have ever known; and, of course, it came from her deep faith in God. In all that she went through, Elizabeth never lost her faith or her joy or her sense of humor.

Some months before her death, Elizabeth had a stem-cell transplant. Her brother, John, was the donor, and John gave so much of himself to her that Elizabeth's blood type actually changed to John's blood type. Jokingly, Elizabeth later told her Sunday school class that before the transplant she had been a vegetarian, but now, with so much of John's blood in her, that she had an intense desire to eat some fried chicken and watch a football game!

Her family, David and Ethel and John and her sister, Alice, said of her, "Elizabeth is the way God meant people to be, a person of joy and love and goodness; a person who is confident in God."

That's number one. Because God loves us, we can choose life; we can choose to live in confidence.

Second, Because God Loves Us, We Can Choose to Live in Gratitude

It was a beautiful spring Saturday afternoon. My wife, June, and I went to eat at one of our favorite barbecue restaurants. We took our plates out to eat at one of the picnic tables on the patio. An attractive family came outside, a mother, a father, and their teenage son. They asked us if the seats just across from us were vacant. The mother had on a Boston Red Sox T-shirt, so I said, "These seats are just for you, but first you have to answer a question: Who won the World Series in 2004?" The woman beamed and said, "The Boston Red Sox, of course!"

They sat down just across from us and performed a fascinating ritual. The father held his fork in the air and said, "Who eats better?" And then, in unison, all three of them said, "Thank you, Lord. Amen."

I said to them, "Tell us about your blessing. What's the story behind that?"

The father smiled and said, "We got that from my wife's granddad! He was so grateful to God for every blessing, so at every meal, no matter what was being served—it could be turkey and dressing and all the trimmings, or cold pork and beans out of a can, or a baloney sandwich on stale bread— he would always do the same thing. He would hold his fork up in the air and say, 'Who eats better?' And we would all say, 'Thank you, Lord. Amen.' It was his way of saying thanks to his wife, who had cooked the meal, and thanks to his God. He just always lived in the spirit of gratitude, so we try to do that too."

This is number two: Because God loves us, we can choose life. We can choose to live first in confidence, and second, in gratitude.

Third and Finally, Because God Loves Us, We Can Choose to Live in Christ

A famous Russian novelist, dramatist, and historian tells of a moment when he was on the verge of giving up all hope as a prisoner in a Soviet prison camp. He was working twelve hours a day at hard labor. He was subsisting on a starvation diet. He had become gravely ill. The doctors were predicting his death; and frankly, he didn't care whether he lived or died.

One afternoon, while shoveling sand under a blazing sun, he simply stopped working. He did so knowing that the guards would beat him severely—perhaps to death. But he didn't care anymore. He felt that he just could not go on. But then he saw another prisoner, a fellow Christian, moving toward him cautiously. With his cane, the man quickly drew a cross in the sand and then quickly erased it.

In that brief moment, the Russian novelist felt all the hope of the gospel flood through his soul. It gave him the strength and courage to endure that difficult day and the hard months of imprisonment that followed.

This man was saved that day by the sign of the cross. That quick reminder of God's love and power gave him the strength to hold on. In the hymn, "Turn Your Eyes Upon Jesus" the hymn writer reminds us that when we look to Jesus, "the things of earth will grow / strangely dim in the light of his glory and grace" (*UM Hymnal*; page 349).

Well, the choice is ours, but let me say to you with all the feeling I have in my heart: Choose life! Because of God's love, because of God's grace, because of God's promise to always be with us, choose to live in confidence, choose to live in gratitude, and choose to live in Christ!

When you make that choice, you will begin to discover the incredible number of amazing, life-changing moments God has in store for you. You will begin to discover everywhere you look and everywhere you go and in everything you do, those amazing, awesome "God-moments" that will take your breath away!

DISCUSSION GUIDE

John D. Schroeder

This book by James W. Moore explores the sorts of powerful, memorable moments in our lives when God breaks into our routines to remind us just how amazing, how wonderful, life truly is.

To assist you in facilitating a small group, this discussion guide was created to help make this experience beneficial for both you and members of your group. Here are some thoughts on how you can help your group:

1. Distribute the book to participants before your first meeting and request that they come having read the first chapter. You may want to limit the size of your group to increase participation.
2. Begin your sessions on time. Your participants will appreciate your promptness. You may wish to begin your first session with introductions and a brief get-acquainted time. Start each session by reading aloud the snapshot summary of the chapter for the day.

3. Select discussion questions and activities in advance. Note that the first question is a general question designed to get discussion going. The last question is designed to summarize the discussion. Feel free to change the order of the listed questions and to create your own questions. Allow a set amount of time for the questions and activities.

4. Remind participants that all questions are valid as part of the learning process. Encourage their participation in discussion by saying there are no "wrong" answers and that all input will be appreciated. Invite participants to share their thoughts, personal stories, and ideas as their comfort level allows.

5. Some questions may be more difficult to answer than others. If you ask a question and no one responds, begin the discussion by venturing an answer yourself. Then ask for comments and other answers. Remember that some questions may have multiple answers.

6. Ask the question "Why?" or "Why do you believe that?" to help continue a discussion and give it greater depth.

7. Give everyone a chance to talk. Keep the conversation moving. Occasionally you may want to direct a question to someone who has been quiet. "Do you have anything to add?" is a good follow-up question to ask another person. If the topic of conversation gets off track, move ahead by asking the next question in your discussion guide.

8. Before moving from questions to activities, ask group members if they have any questions that have not been answered. Remember that as a leader, you do not have to know all the answers. Some answers may come from group members. Other answers may even need a bit of research. Your job is to keep the discussion moving and to encourage participation.

9. Review the activity in advance. Feel free to modify it or to create your own activity. Encourage participants to try the "At home" activity.
10. Following the conclusion of the activity, close with a brief prayer, praying either the printed prayer from the discussion guide or a prayer of your own. If your group desires, pause for individual prayer petitions.
11. Be grateful and supportive. Thank group members for their ideas and participation.
12. You are not expected to be a "perfect" leader. Just do the best you can by focusing on the participants and the lesson. God will help you lead this group.
13. Enjoy your time together!

Suggestions for Participants

1. What you will receive from this discussion group will be in direct proportion to your involvement. Be an active participant!
2. Please make it a point to attend all sessions and to arrive on time so that you can receive the greatest benefit.
3. Read the chapter and review the discussion guide questions prior to the meeting. You may want to jot down questions you have from the reading and also answers to some of the discussion guide questions.
4. Be supportive and appreciative of your group leader as well as the other members of your group. You are on a journey together.
5. Your participation is encouraged. Feel free to share your thoughts about the material being discussed.
6. Pray for your group and your leader.

Chapter 1
It's Not the Number of Breaths We Take, But the Number of Moments That Take Our Breath Away

SNAPSHOT SUMMARY: *This chapter examines life's breathtaking moments of love, gratitude, and inspiration.*

Reflection / Discussion Questions

1. Share why you decided to read this book. What do you hope to gain from this experience?
2. How does it feel to experience a breathtaking moment? Do such moments always literally have to take your breath away? Explain your answer.
3. Describe a particular moment in your life that took your breath away.
4. What do breathtaking moments have in common?
5. Why do people long-remember a breathtaking moment?
6. Share a moment of love that took your breath away.
7. Recall a time when you were the giver or receiver of a moment of gratitude.
8. Name some special moments that inspire people.
9. Why are moments of breathtaking inspiration important?
10. What do breathtaking moments reveal about God?

Activities

• *As a group:* Search the Bible for breathtaking moments.

• *At home:* Make a list of breathtaking moments you have experienced.

Prayer: *Dear God, thank you for the moments in life that take our breath away. Help us to cherish these special times and remember your love for us. Amen.*

Chapter 2
The Moments When We Know We Are Standing on Holy Ground

SNAPSHOT SUMMARY: *This chapter reminds us that holy ground is all around us, including the holy ground of service, love, and sacred responsibility.*

Reflection / Discussion Questions

1. Explain what it means to be standing on holy ground.
2. What lessons can be found in the story of Moses and the burning bush?
3. Share a time when you felt the presence of God or when you felt you were being called.
4. As Christians, what is our calling? What does God expect from us?
5. Name some Christian vocations. Can you serve God in any type of work? Explain.
6. Reflect on / discuss what is meant by "the holy ground of love."
7. Reflect on / discuss how and why Jesus expects us to love one another.
8. What is meant by "sacred responsibility"? Give an example.
9. Name some of the ways in which God speaks to us.
10. What additional thoughts or ideas from this chapter would you like to explore?

Activities

• *As a group:* Create a constant reminder that you are called by God. Create your own "I Am Called to..." calling card that you can carry with you or place in a special spot at work or home. Share the meaning behind your card with the other members of your group.

• *At home:* Reflect upon how you have been called by God and the opportunities you have to serve God each day.

Prayer: *Dear God, thank you for the joy and opportunity to stand upon your holy ground and to serve others. Help us to be faithful to our calling. Amen.*

Chapter 3
The Moments When We Say, "Ah"

SNAPSHOT SUMMARY: *This chapter looks at the "ahs" and the "blahs" of life. It reminds us that "blah" moments are temporary, that we can make use of such low moments, that we can learn to see the "ah" moments all around us, that we can attack the "blahs" with a positive faith, and that there is an outside source of strength.*

Reflection / Discussion Questions

1. Share one of the "ah" moments of life you have experienced.
2. What are some of the "blahs" of life that most people experience?
3. How did the apostle Paul handle the troubles he faced?
4. Give an example of a temporary "blah" that you had recently.
5. Reflect on / discuss some of the different ways and strategies to make high use of low moments.
6. What is needed in order to see the "ah" things of life?
7. Describe how an "ah" moment feels. Compare it to the feeling of a "blah" moment.

8. Brainstorm ways to attack the "blahs" with a positive faith.

9. Why is it important to remember your outside source of strength?

10. What additional thoughts or ideas from this chapter would you like to explore?

Activities

• *As a group:* If you were to put together a "Fight the Blahs Kit," what would you include in it? Together, make a list of things to fight the "blahs."

• *At home:* Reflect upon the ups and downs of your life. Can you see the hand of God in those moments? How will you prepare for the "blahs" that may come?

Prayer: *Dear God, thank you for being with us in the ups and downs of life. Help us to remember that you are always with us. Amen.*

Chapter 4
The Moments When God Meets Us With His Lovingkindness at Every Corner

SNAPSHOT SUMMARY: *This chapter shows how God is with us at "the dropping-off place," in the places of darkness and trouble, and at the place of death.*

Reflection / Discussion Questions

1. Share a moment when God met you with lovingkindness.

2. Describe some of the many ways God shows lovingkindness.

3. How does it feel to know God is with us at all times?

4. Reread Psalm 139:7-12. How does this passage speak to you?
5. Name some of "the dropping-off places" in life.
6. Reflect on / discuss how God ministers to us in times of darkness and trouble.
7. Why can we be confident in the face of death?
8. Brainstorm ways to remember that God is always with us.
9. How should we respond to God's lovingkindness?
10. What additional thoughts or ideas from this chapter would you like to explore?

Activities

• *As a group:* Make a list of some of the promises and kindnesses of God.

• *At home:* Count the ways and times that God has shown kindness to you. Show kindness to a stranger this week.

Prayer: *Dear God, thank you for the lovingkindness you give so freely. Help us to show the same lovingkindness to others. Amen.*

Chapter 5
The Moments When We Move Forward, Trusting God

SNAPSHOT SUMMARY: *This chapter offers encouragement to move forward and not to look back on past successes, past hurts, or past failures.*

Reflection / Discussion Questions

1. Share a time when you moved forward, trusting God.
2. Reflect on / discuss what often prevents people from moving forward in trust.

3. Give some reasons why we can trust God.

4. Why is it often dangerous to look back and not ahead?

5. Reflect on / discuss how and why success can ruin some people.

6. What are some of the hurts in life that many people experience?

7. When you look back at past hurts, what can happen to you?

8. Why can recalling past failures be harmful?

9. List ideas and strategies for keeping a trusting, forward focus.

10. What additional thoughts or ideas from this chapter would you like to explore?

Activities

• *As a group:* Let each group member write a spiritual affirmation based upon this chapter. Share and explain your affirmations.

• *At home:* Reflect upon your trust in God. Walk in faith with God this week.

Prayer: *Dear God, thank you for trust in you, which allows us to move forward in life. Help us always to focus on you now and in the future. Amen.*

Chapter 6
The Moments When God Gives Us the Strength to Rise Above Bitterness

SNAPSHOT SUMMARY: *This chapter examines what it means to "go the second mile." This includes overcoming evil with good, always doing more than expected, taking responsibility for your own attitudes, and living daily in the spirit of Christ.*

Reflection / Discussion Questions

1. Without warning, life can compel us to face a problem. Give some examples.
2. Share a time when you dealt with a difficult situation.
3. What choices do people have when compelled to face unwanted situations?
4. What are some of the dangers of bitterness?
5. What did Jesus mean by going the second mile?
6. Reflect on / discuss ways to overcome evil with good.
7. List and discuss the author's "three possible ways of doing things." Why is it best to do more than what is expected?
8. Why is it important to take responsibility for your own attitudes?
9. Share some ways we can live daily in the spirit of Christ.
10. What additional thoughts or ideas from this chapter would you like to explore?

Activities

• *As a group:* Create a list of keys to going the second mile. Talk about your list, and see if you can agree on which suggestions are the best.

OR

• *As a group:* Create a list of some antidotes for bitterness.

• *At home:* Go the extra mile for someone this week.

Prayer: *Dear God, thank you for giving us the strength to rise above bitterness. Help us to go the extra mile for others and to live daily in the spirit of Christ. Amen.*

Chapter 7
The Moments When Faith Overcomes Doubt

SNAPSHOT SUMMARY: This chapter looks at what produces a doubter. Reasons include that some people doubt because they are dropouts, some choose to be negative, some mistakenly assume that the only truth is scientific truth, and some are afraid to make a leap of faith.

Reflection / Discussion Questions

1. Share a time when you struggled between doubt and faith.
2. Why do people doubt? Give reasons why we sometimes lack faith.
3. Do you believe it is easier to doubt or easier to have faith? Explain your answer.
4. Reflect on / discuss the connection between doubt and being a dropout.
5. Why do some people choose to be negative? What are they missing?
6. Why did Thomas doubt? Give some reasons for his lack of faith.
7. Name some important truths that cannot be scientifically documented.
8. Reflect on / discuss reasons why some people are afraid to make a personal commitment.
9. In your own words, explain what it means to take a "leap of faith."
10. What additional thoughts or ideas from this chapter would you like to explore?

Activities

• *As a group:* Create a list of the top ten reasons why faith is stronger than doubt.

OR

• *As a group:* Reflect upon your faith, and in a few sentences, write down what faith means to you. Share your response with the group.

• *At home:* Reflect upon your own struggles between doubt and faith. Take a leap of faith this week.

Prayer: *Dear God, thank you for a faith that overcomes doubt. Help us to take a leap of faith and learn to trust in your love and goodness. Amen.*

Chapter 8
The Moments When God Redeems Our Troubles

SNAPSHOT SUMMARY: *This chapter reminds us of breathtaking things to remember when we are faced with trouble, including that God is with us, God can redeem our troubles, and God can use us to help others who are in trouble.*

Reflection / Discussion Questions

1. What impresses you about the way people responded in a positive manner to the trouble created by Hurricane Katrina?
2. Share a time when you were able to face trouble with help from God or others.
3. Describe some of the different responses people may have when facing trouble. What choices do we have in how we respond?
4. "God is with us"; explain what this promise means to you.

5. Reflect on / discuss why we can trust God in times of trouble.

6. Explain how and why redeeming our troubles—using them—is a key to Christian living.

7. What can we learn from how Jesus faced trouble?

8. How can we help others who are in trouble? Name some of the ways people can be of help.

9. Compare how it feels to be in trouble with how it feels when trouble is over.

10. What additional thoughts or ideas from this chapter would you like to explore?

Activities

• *As a group:* Locate and share favorite Bible verses that give you help in times of trouble.

• *At home:* This week, assist someone who is in trouble and who needs your help.

Prayer: *Dear God, thank you for redeeming us from our troubles. Help us to remember that you are always with us and that help is only a prayer away. Amen.*

Chapter 9
The Moments of Responsive Gratitude

SNAPSHOT SUMMARY: *This chapter illustrates responsive gratitude by showing how Christ gave Zacchaeus a new appreciation, a new set of priorities, and a new motivation.*

Reflection / Discussion Questions

1. Share what "responsive gratitude" means to you.

2. What often makes people unable to see and appreciate miracles?
3. What is spiritual blindness, and what is the cure for it?
4. Describe how it feels to be grateful.
5. Share a time when you felt gratitude to God for a blessing.
6. What lessons can we learn from the story of Zacchaeus?
7. Why do we all need a new appreciation like the kind Jesus gave to Zacchaeus?
8. What kinds of new motivation and priorities did Jesus instill in Zacchaeus?
9. Brainstorm ways we can enhance our spirit of gratitude.
10. What additional thoughts or ideas from this chapter would you like to explore?

Activities

• *As a group:* Write brief prayers of thanksgiving. Share your prayers among the group.

• *At home:* Count your blessings this week, and seek out ways to be a blessing to others.

Prayer: *Dear God, thank you for blessing us so richly. Help us to respond in gratitude. Open our eyes to the miracles all around us, that we may reach out in love to others. Amen.*

Chapter 10
The Moments When the Holy Spirit Uses Us

SNAPSHOT SUMMARY: This chapter shows how the Holy Spirit melts us, molds us, fills us, and uses us.

Reflection / Discussion Questions

1. Reflect on / discuss why Jesus sent the Holy Spirit to the disciples.
2. Why did the disciples have to become like little children before they could receive the Holy Spirit?
3. Share a time when you felt the presence of God's Holy Spirit. In what ways has the Holy Spirit used you to fulfill God's purposes?
4. Compare the situation of the disciples before and after they received the Holy Spirit.
5. Explain what is meant by the statement, "God's way is not to break hearts, but to melt them."
6. How have you been shaped and changed by the Holy Spirit?
7. Reflect on / discuss how the redeeming love of God can change the human heart.
8. What happens when the Holy Spirit fills us? What changes take place?
9. Reflect on / discuss what people need to do to receive the Holy Spirit into their life.
10. What additional thoughts or ideas from this chapter would you like to explore?

Activities

• *As a group:* Draw pictures or symbols that represent the Holy Spirit. Share your illustrations among the group.

• *At home:* Reflect upon how the Holy Spirit has touched your life.

Prayer: *Dear God, thank you for giving us moments when the Holy Spirit uses us. Help us to allow the Holy Spirit to melt us, mold us, fill us, and use us for your glory. Amen.*

Chapter 11
The Moments When We Truly Celebrate Life

SNAPSHOT SUMMARY: *This chapter shows how to make each day count by being aware, by doing something for someone else, and by trusting God for tomorrow.*

Reflection / Discussion Questions

1. Give some reasons why life should be celebrated.
2. What do people often miss when they look to the past or future, but not the present?
3. Give some reasons why life may be passing some people by.
4. Give some reasons why each day and moment are special.
5. Name some things that often get in the way of enjoying life.
6. Reflect on / discuss how being more aware can help make each day count.
7. What causes people to be insensitive rather than aware?
8. List some simple things we can do for others that make a big difference.
9. What can we learn from the life of Jesus about making each day count?
10. What additional thoughts or ideas from this chapter would you like to explore?

Activities

• *As a group:* List the benefits of doing something for others.
OR
• *As a group:* We celebrate birthdays and anniversaries; how do we celebrate life? Brainstorm ways to live in the now and to celebrate life just as it is.

• *At home:* Take a moment this week to celebrate your life in a creative manner.

Prayer: *Dear God, thank you for the joys and celebrations of life. Help us to make each day count and to be thankful for all the blessings you provide. Amen.*

Chapter 12
The Moments When We Realize That God Really Does Love Us

SNAPSHOT SUMMARY: *This chapter shows how we can choose to live in confidence, in gratitude, and in Christ, because God loves us just as we are.*

Reflection / Discussion Questions

1. Share a story of love that has made an impact on you.
2. What are some of the important choices people make each day.
3. How can the Christian faith help us choose to celebrate life?
4. Reread Deuteronomy 30:15-20, and reflect on / discuss what Moses has to say to the Israelites.
5. Describe some ways in which we choose life with God.
6. How does a person live with confidence? What does a confident life based upon faith in God look like?
7. What does it mean to live in gratitude? Give an example.
8. How would you explain to someone what it means to live in Christ?
9. Share how you have been changed by God's love.
10. What additional thoughts or ideas from this chapter would you like to explore?

Activities

• *As a group:* Create Bible bookmarks that remind you that God's love for us is real and everlasting.

• *At home:* Reflect upon your experience of reading this book and sharing with other members of your group. Consider how you would like to apply what you have gained in your daily life.

Prayer: *Dear God, thank you for loving us just as we are. Help us to go forward in life with a deeper appreciation of the moments that take our breath away. Amen.*